The LIGHT and the LIFE

Ardeth G. Kapp · Judith S. Smith

Bookcraft

SALT LAKE CITY, UTAH

Library of Congress Catalog Card Number: 84-73524
ISBN 0-88494-559-6

First Printing, 1985

Printed in the United States of America

He marked the path and led the way,
And every point defines
To light and life and endless day
Where God's full presence shines.

—Eliza R. Snow.

CONTENTS

PREFACE

It was in March 1980 that we first considered the possibility of writing a book in narrative style relating the life and mission of the Savior. A question weighed heavily upon us: Would it be appropriate to attempt such a work? In November 1982 we again discussed, this time more earnestly, the responsibility of such a project. The weeks that followed were filled with humble petitions and searching and study. We determined that the work should be undertaken and committed ourselves to the project.

While this writing would be but a brief sketch of the life of the greatest one who ever walked the earth, we worked with the hope that the events selected would be reported with integrity both in fact and feeling. Our desire was to lead readers to acquire a thirsting that would draw them to the original source, the word of God recorded in the scriptures themselves, and that the scholarly would find nothing to offend or detract in the simple, straightforward style of the writing. We hoped the selected events would convey an overview of the life and mission of the Savior and of the reader's relationship to those events both past and present.

The LDS scriptures, with their masterful, comprehensive references, were the source and foundation for our work. The chronology we have used is based primarily on the great contribution of President J. Reuben Clark, Jr., *Our Lord of the Gospels.* We express gratitude for the unparalleled works by two apostles, *Jesus the Christ,* by Elder James E. Talmage, and the six volumes on the Messiah, by Elder Bruce R. McConkie. Our preparation and research brought us to the writings of F. W. Farrar (*The*

Life of Christ, 1874) and Alfred Edersheim (*The Life and Times of Jesus the Messiah,* 1883), whose unique talents and backgrounds give precious keys to an understanding of the conditions in the Savior's day and of his teachings. We found extremely helpful the manuals prepared for the various institute courses by the Church Educational System. The careful reporting of the progress of the Church and the general conference addresses and other messages of the living prophets by the *Ensign* magazine were valuable resources.

It is our earnest desire that as these pages are read, they will stand as a testimony of the Lord Jesus Christ, and that they will increase the commitment in every reader's heart to study the Savior's life and words contained in the holy scriptures and accept his invitation to every soul to partake of light and life.

ACKNOWLEDGMENTS

The writing of this book could not have been accomplished without the sustaining influence and patient support of our companions and family members—Heber Kapp, Sharon G. Larsen, and David, Becky, Mark, and Sven Smith. To them we express our deepest appreciation.

Though we alone accept the full responsibility for this writing, we gratefully acknowledge the effort expended and the valuable suggestions given by the adults and youth who critiqued the manuscript; the timely encouragement of our friend Vivian Paulsen; and the expertise and kindly guidance of George Bickerstaff.

SOURCES QUOTED OR REFERRED TO

Bryant S. Hinckley, comp., *Sermons and Missionary Services of Melvin J. Ballard.* Salt Lake City: Deseret Book Company, 1949.

Cowley, Matthias F., *Wilford Woodruff: History of His Life and Labors.* Salt Lake City: Bookcraft, 1964.

Edersheim, Alfred, *The Life and Times of Jesus the Messiah.* Grand Rapids, Michigan: Wm. B. Eerdmans Publishing, 1981.

History of the Church, 7 vols.

Kimball, Spencer W., *Spencer W. Kimball Speaks Out.* Salt Lake City: Deseret Book Company, 1981.

McConkie, Bruce R., *Doctrinal New Testament Commentary.* 3 vols. Salt Lake City: Bookcraft, 1973.

McConkie, Bruce R., *The Mortal Messiah.* 4 vols. Salt Lake City: Deseret Book Company, 1981.

Smith, Joseph, *Teachings of the Prophet Joseph Smith,* Joseph Fielding Smith, comp. Salt Lake City: Deseret Book Company, 1977.

Talmage, James E., *Jesus the Christ.* Salt Lake City: Deseret Book Company, 1949.

Talmage, James E., *A Study of the Articles of Faith.* Salt Lake City: The Church of Jesus Christ of Latter-day Saints, 1977.

Sidon

Tyre

Mt. Her[]

Transfiguration
Boy with evil spirit []

Caesarea
Philippi

Peter testifies

Galilee

Plain of Gennesaret
Many healed

Capernaum

Bread of Life sermon

Bethsaida

Feeding of five thousan[]

Sea of
Galilee

Walks on the sea

Samaria

Ephraim

Indefinite period of time
spent with apostles
Final circuit towards
Jerusalem begins

Perea

Feast of the Tabernacles
Blind man healed
"Light of the World"
testimony
Good Shepherd parable
Feast of dedication

Mustard seed parable
Begins journey towards
Jerusalem
Message that Lazarus
is sick
Meal with Pharisees
Goes before twelve towards
Jerusalem

Jerusalem

Bethany

Visits Mary and Martha
Raising of Lazarus
Plot against Jesus
Retires to Ephraim

Judea

Chapter 1

THE WAITING WORLD

No doubt he was not the only baby born in Bethlehem that year, or even that month or week. But he was the only one whose birth was heralded by an angel, marked by the appearance of a new star, and proclaimed by heavenly choirs.

The great anticipation of this event—the birth of the Savior and Redeemer of the world—began long ago. It began when Jesus Christ spoke in the great council that was held in heaven. We were there. Jesus was there with the Father. And Lucifer, another of the sons of God who was a mighty spirit and a persuasive leader, was also there. In this council, our Father in Heaven presented his plan for all of his children to come to the earth, to receive mortal bodies, and to work out their salvation. After the plan was explained, a great shout of joy went up from those who were assembled. (See Job 38:7.) We were eager and excited to take this great step—to progress and become more like our Father in Heaven.

It was explained that our earth experience would be a test. We would be free to choose between good and evil and to see if we would be true to the commandments our Father in Heaven had given us. (See Abraham 3:24–26.) Because our Father knew that all of us would make mistakes—mistakes that would keep us from his presence—he planned to provide a Savior for us. If we would repent of them, this Savior would atone for our sins and he would show us by the example of his own earth life how we could be redeemed and return to live with our Father in Heaven. Now the central issue of the council was at hand, and Heavenly Father asked, "Whom shall I send?"

Jesus spoke. His whole personage radiated the love he felt for each of our Father in Heaven's children. Knowing fully that to follow the Father's plan and atone for our sins he must suffer and die for us, he said "Here am I, send me." (Abraham 3:27.) In this he willingly chose to be obedient and to serve his Heavenly Father: "Father, thy will be done, and the glory be thine forever."

Lucifer now spoke: "Behold, here am I, send me." But Lucifer proposed to change the plan. "I will redeem all mankind, that one soul shall not be lost." His plan would not allow God's children to choose between good and evil during their mortal life; instead Lucifer planned to force us to be obedient in order to return to heaven. Furthermore, he wanted to claim the power and glory of the Father. He said, "Surely I will do it; wherefore give me thine honor." (See Moses 4:1–2.)

There was a feeling of great discord and disharmony as Lucifer finished. Because Lucifer would have taken away our free agency, and because he selfishly sought God's power, he was rejected. Our Father in Heaven chose Jesus to be our Savior.

Lucifer became very angry. When he could not have his way, he rebelled against God and Jesus Christ. He used all of his strength to persuade others to follow him. He was powerful and eloquent. Heavenly Father's children were faced with a choice.

The great love of our Father in Heaven and his Son drew to them all of us who would later be sent to earth. We understood the plan that had been presented, and its truth brought feelings of peace and the joyous anticipation of progress. We wanted to be valiant and faithful. We reaffirmed our acceptance of the plan, and we determined to follow Jesus Christ and walk with him, no matter how hard the path.

Nevertheless, Lucifer was able to persuade others of Heavenly Father's children to believe in him. Because he and the spirits who chose to follow him were no longer in harmony with God's laws, they were cast out of heaven and were denied the great blessing of obtaining a mortal body. They came to the earth determined to destroy God's plan and to lead his faithful children into paths of evil. Satan would do all in his power to keep these faithful ones from discovering the truth of the gospel, to destroy their faith in God, and to make them follow him. (See D&C 76:25—29.)

In the premortal life our Father in Heaven and Jesus Christ called and ordained many of the strongest spirits to be sent to the earth during specific time periods or dispensations. (See D&C 138:53—56.) These the Lord trusted to recognize the truths they had been taught before and to become his followers, leaders, and prophets on the earth. Their most vital responsibility would be to teach the people of the birth and mission of Jesus Christ and the plan for their salvation.

Adam was the first valiant spirit chosen by our Father in Heaven to come to the earth and become a great prophet leader. Enoch, Noah, Abraham, Moses, and many others would follow. So that Adam and his children after him would better understand the coming birth and mission of Jesus Christ, the Lord commanded them to offer the firstborn animals of their flocks as an offering to him. This was symbolic of the sacrifice that Jesus would make for us when he would come to the earth and atone for our sins. By voluntarily giving his own life, the Savior would redeem every child of God who accepted his gospel. (See Moses 5:4—12.)

As time passed Satan did all in his power to keep the people of the earth from listening to the prophets and learning of God's plan and the coming of his Son. But in spite of the wickedness and war Satan inspired around him, the prophet Enoch led a group of people to be so obedient that the Lord called them Zion. Because of their love for the Lord and his gospel, they achieved a unity of heart and purpose. Enoch's people received a fullness of joy, and they walked with God again. (See Moses 7:18—19, 69.)

During the time that Noah lived on the earth, Satan's influence increased. He and his angels rejoiced. But as the Lord saw his children losing their love for each other, being filled with hate, and willfully choosing to follow Satan, he wept. He loved all his children and wanted them to be happy. He longed for them to understand that they could repent of their sins, accept the gospel, believe in his Son who would come, and return to live with him.

With great love and patience, the Lord instructed the prophet Noah to keep teaching the people. Though his life was in danger, Noah labored for over a hundred years to persuade them to change. He taught and pleaded with them: "Believe and repent of your sins and be baptized in the name of Jesus Christ, the Son of God, even as our fathers, and ye shall receive the Holy Ghost; . . . and if ye do not this, the floods will come in upon you."

Because they were proud and thought themselves self-sufficient, the people would not listen to the Lord's prophet. They had made the popular choice; their very thoughts had become "evil continually." And while they were going about their daily acts, they were overtaken and destroyed by the flood that cleansed the entire earth. (See Moses 8:22–30.)

Generations passed and the Lord sent one of his strongest spirits to the earth. His name was Abraham. Though his father worshipped idols, Abraham was determined to walk in faith and to follow every instruction the Lord gave him. (See Abraham 1:2–5.) The Lord proved Abraham and found him faithful to every test. He then knew that he could depend on Abraham and that Abraham would also teach his children to follow Him.

Through Abraham the Lord was able to establish a covenant people. Abraham became known as the father of the faithful. Abraham's son Isaac and Isaac's son Jacob were also obedient and made covenants to keep the Lord's commandments. They faithfully obeyed the gospel, offered sacrifices, and looked forward to the coming of Jesus Christ. Jacob's name was changed to Israel, and his descendants became known as the children of Israel. The Lord promised in the covenant he made with Abraham that all those who accept the gospel and are true to it will become members of the house of Israel in eternity and heirs to the blessings of eternal life, the greatest of all the gifts of God. (See Abraham 2:9–11.)

Over the following centuries, the children of Israel had many struggles. They were greatly influenced by the idol-worshipping nations around them. In Egypt they were enslaved by Pharaoh. The Lord called Moses to deliver them from this bondage. (See Moses 1:25—26.) Though the Israelites were disobedient, the Lord did not withdraw his love. He performed great miracles for them —parting the Red Sea for their escape, and providing water, manna, and quail for their food as they travelled in the wilderness toward the land of Palestine, which would become their home.

The Lord longed to come to the Israelites and teach them personally. Moses tried to prepare the children of Israel to see the Lord and receive his laws, but they hardened their hearts. They even fashioned a golden calf to worship instead of the living God. (See Exodus 20:18—21; 32:1—9.)

Because of their lack of faith, the Israelites pulled away from the Lord, and since they could only receive and live a lesser law than the gospel, a law of performances and ordinances, that is what the Lord gave them. This law became known as the law of Moses. (See Mosiah 13:29—33.) The people lost the privilege of receiving the Melchizedek Priesthood, but the Aaronic or Levitical Priesthood, established to administer these lesser ordinances, continued with them. (See JST, Exodus 34:1—2.)

Israel was permitted to have first a tabernacle and later a temple for their worship of the Lord. But just as they had not prepared themselves to go before the Lord personally in Moses' day, they could not approach him personally in the temple. Only the priests, descendants of Moses' brother, Aaron, could officiate there and represent the people to the Lord. The duties of the priests included the offering of sacrifices.

In spite of their hardheartedness, the Lord mercifully continued to send his prophets to the children of Israel to warn them and to teach them again to look forward to the coming of his Son. Isaiah, Ezekiel, Micah, and Zechariah all prophesied of the coming Messiah, Jesus Christ, who would deliver them from sin through his atonement. But Israel was not faithful. The nation as a whole would not heed the prophets' call to repentance and they did not honor their covenants. Because they chose to walk in the ways of the world instead of the ways of the Lord, they lost his protection and were oppressed by other nations. Twice they were taken into bondage—by Assyria and Babylon.

After many years in captivity, some of the Israelites of the former kingdom of Judah were permitted to return to Jerusalem from the Babylonian captivity and rebuild the temple. (See Ezra 1:1—5.) These people began to gather together the writings of the prophets and the first five books of the Bible, which contained the law of Moses, but without living prophets and revelation to guide them, the religious rulers of the people became divided into groups. Some of these groups were the Pharisees and the Sadducees. Each applied the law differently, and each tried to persuade the people to accept its own views.

The true spirit of the laws and ordinances that God had given so long ago to prophets such as Adam, Enoch, Noah, Abraham, and Moses to prepare for the coming of his Son was lost to the majority of the people.

Then one day, in the city of Jerusalem, a very old priest who held the Aaronic priesthood prepared to take his turn in officiating at the temple. It was a very sacred opportunity—an opportunity he would probably have only once in his life. During his lifetime he had been faithful to the commandments of the Lord. He and his wife had not been blessed with children, but he had learned to place the Lord's will ahead of all other things. Quietly, prayerfully, Zacharias now entered the Holy Place to burn incense on the golden altar.

Suddenly an angel of the Lord appeared before him. He was frightened and amazed. With gentle reassurance, the heavenly messenger spoke these marvelous words of comfort and promise: "Fear not, Zacharias: for thy prayer is heard; and thy wife Elisabeth shall bear thee a son.

"He shall . . . make ready a people prepared for the Lord" (Luke 1:13, 17).

The long waiting of the faithful of all ages past was over. The angel had promised Zacharias a son, who would be called John. This promised son would be the forerunner, the prophet who would prepare the people for the coming of Jesus Christ, the Son of God. (See 1 Nephi 10:7–10.)

Chapter 2

"UNTO YOU IS BORN . . . A SAVIOUR"

The people waited anxiously at the temple in Jerusalem in the place of the general assembly. They had seen the smoke rising from the burning incense. But why was the priest, Zacharias, so long in returning to give the benediction?

When Zacharias finally came out, he only motioned to the restless congregation, for he could not speak. A miraculous sign was given to Zacharias to remove all doubt that what the angel had announced would truly come to pass. The angel told him that he would be struck dumb until his promised son was born and given the name of John.

Realizing that Zacharias had seen a vision, but dismissed by his gestures, the people wondered over these unusual events as they made their way out of the temple court and into the crowded streets of Jerusalem. Zacharias too, was filled with awe and excitement. On finishing his temple service, he left the crowded city and hurried toward his home in the Judean hills to share this wondrous experience with his beloved Elisabeth.

A few months later another marvelous revelation occurred. This time it was in the north, far from the splendor of the temple at Jerusalem. Here lay the little city of Nazareth in Galilee. Here the same heavenly messenger, Gabriel, was sent by God to a beautiful young woman named Mary.

The angel greeted Mary with words of praise and assurance, declaring that she was "highly favoured," and blessed among women. Mary was troubled and amazed at this greeting, and her mind filled with questions.

The messenger spoke reassuringly: "Fear not, Mary: for thou hast found favour with God. And, behold, thou shalt . . . bring forth a son, and shalt call his name JESUS." The angel also told Mary that Jesus would reign over the house of Jacob (Israel) forever, and that his kingdom should have no end.

Mary had a knowledge of the foretold Messiah, who would be born of the royal line. But she could hardly grasp the wondrous meaning of the messenger's words. And how would this come about? She was not yet married, though she was pledged to Joseph, the carpenter. Humbly, Mary asked the angel how she could have a son, not being married. Then the heavenly messenger explained that Mary's child was to be the Son of God.

As Mary tried to grasp this overwhelming message, the angel continued with another marvelous announcement. "Behold, thy cousin, Elisabeth . . . hath also conceived a son in her old age: and this is the sixth month with her, who was called barren." And then followed the simple, eternal truth: "For with God nothing shall be impossible."

The visit from an angel sent by the Lord filled Mary's heart with trust and faith. She responded, "Behold the handmaid of the Lord; be it unto me according to thy word."

The angel departed, and Mary was left alone. Thoughts, prayers, feelings swept over her as she recalled over and over the angel's message: "That . . . which shall be born of thee shall be called the Son of God." (See Luke 1:28—38.) Later, seeking companionship and understanding, she went to confide her sacred message to her cousin Elisabeth.

Mary spent several weeks at the home of Elisabeth and Zacharias in the Judean hills. There they must have shared sacred moments together as they pondered the scriptures and the glorious prophecies which were about to come true. They marvelled and wanted to be ready and worthy of the great honor that the Lord had bestowed on them, his handmaidens.

It was difficult for the young Mary to leave the comfort and companionship of her much older cousin. Both Mary's and Elisabeth's condition had served as a testimony to strengthen each other. But now Mary must return to her own home in Nazareth, and how would she tell her espoused husband, Joseph?

Joseph, the carpenter, was a just man and worthy of revelation. When he became aware of Mary's condition, he wondered about the future of their relationship and what he should do. He was blessed with a dream in which an angel appeared to him. The angel addressed him saying, "Joseph, thou son of David," for Joseph was a descendant of the great King David of Israel. Mary was also a descendant of the same royal lineage. (See James E. Talmage, *Jesus the Christ*, Salt Lake City: Deseret Book

Company, 1974, pp. 85—87; hereinafter referred to as *Jesus the Christ.*)

The angel reassured Joseph and instructed him not to be afraid but to go ahead with the marriage. He then explained that Mary's child would be a son, that he was to be named Jesus, and would "save his people from their sins." (See Matthew 1:20—25.) When Joseph realized that Mary, whom he loved, was to be the mother of the Savior of the world, he quickly did as the angel instructed. By marriage he gave Mary protection and became the lawful guardian of the child.

It was early spring when Joseph and Mary's quiet life together was intruded upon by the edict of Rome. Though the Jewish people had survived captivity, they did not have self-government and were at that time a province of the Roman Empire. Caesar Augustus required that a census be taken in order to levy taxes on his vast dominions. Herod the Great, the hated, Roman-appointed king of Judea, was to carry out this order. Thus Joseph and Mary made the long journey from Nazareth to Bethlehem (their ancestral home) to be enrolled in the Roman census.

On reaching Bethlehem, weary from their travel, they found the city crowded, and to their dismay, the inn was already filled with people from the outlying districts who had also come to register. Joseph and Mary took shelter in the only available space—a stable. "And so it was, that, while they were there, the days were accomplished that she should be delivered. And she brought forth her first-born son, and wrapped him in swaddling clothes, and laid him in a manger" (Luke 2:6—7). On this first Christmas, Jesus, the Son of God, began his earthly mission by being born in a humble stable. During this holy night, God the Father gave to the world the greatest of all Christmas gifts. He sent his Son to the earth to become our Savior and Redeemer.

Outside the city, not far from this sacred scene, some shepherds were quietly watching their flocks. The night air was cool around them, and the heavens shimmered with stars. Suddenly, they found themselves bathed in light as the angel of the Lord stood before them declaring this joyous message: "Unto you is born this day in the city of David a Saviour, which is Christ the Lord." The messenger gave them a sign by which they would recognize the child. "Ye shall find the babe wrapped in swaddling clothes, lying in a manger." Then it seemed as if the veil were withdrawn, and the shepherds saw and heard a "multitude of the heavenly host," praising God and declaring peace and good will to men on earth. Many, both on earth and in heaven, who had looked forward to the coming of the Son of God, rejoiced on this night of his birth.

After this remarkable experience, the shepherds went immediately into the city. There they found Mary and Joseph "and the babe lying in a manger," just as the angel had declared. Having heard the glorious news, they now saw for themselves. They knew that prophecy was being fulfilled that night and that the newborn child was the promised Son of God. When they returned to their flock, they were filled with joy and praised God. They began to tell others of the angel's message and bore testimony of the birth of the Savior. (See Luke 2:8—17.)

A few days after Jesus' birth, Joseph and Mary made the short journey from Bethlehem to the temple in Jerusalem to fulfil requirements of the law of Moses. While they were there, Simeon, a devoted Israelite, was prompted by the Spirit to come to the temple. The Holy Ghost had revealed to Simeon that he would not die until he had seen Christ. He had patiently held the Lord's promise close through many seasons. As he came into the temple and saw Joseph and Mary with the baby, he recognized in the child the promised Messiah. The old man gathered the baby into his arms and praised God and blessed Joseph and Mary. Simeon was joined by Anna, a widow and a prophetess. Anna was a righteous woman in tune with the whisperings of the Spirit, and she too recognized the Redeemer and rejoiced in his birth. Later, she testified of him to all those about her in Jerusalem. (See Luke 2:22–38.)

Joseph and Mary marvelled at all that was said about the child, each still trying to comprehend all that had taken place in the months past. They began their return home, wondering but in peace, while Jerusalem was left questioning and disturbed. There were rumors that prophecy was being fulfilled—that a child had been born who was destined to become the king of the Jews.

Most disturbed was wicked King Herod of Judea. Months had passed since the beginning of the rumors, but now there stood before him wise men who had come from the east to his court and who asked openly and simply, "Where is he that is born King of the Jews? for we have seen his star in the east, and are come to worship him."

Herod had defended what he perceived as threats to his throne at the price of blood, even the lives of his own wife and several sons. Jealousy and suspicion raged in him at the thought that his rule was again threatened. But his cunning prevailed as he called together the chief priests and scribes and demanded to know where this prophesied Christ would be born. They answered, "In Bethlehem of Judaea," and quoted to him the words of the prophet

Micah who had lived seven hundred years earlier: "But thou, Beth-lehem, . . . out of thee shall he come forth unto me that is to be ruler in Israel" (Micah 5:2).

Herod dismissed them and summoned the wise men privately. His evil scheme unfolded as he asked them to tell him when the star had appeared. Then he told the wise men that they should go to Bethlehem and "search diligently for the young child; and when ye have found him, bring me word again, that I may come and worship him also."

As the wise men left Jerusalem to continue their quest, they again caught sight of the new star. They found the house where Joseph and Mary were living, and when they saw the young child, Jesus, they fell on their knees and worshipped him. They presented him with gold, frankincense, and myrrh, gifts appropriate for a king. Like the shepherds before them, and Simeon and Anna, the wise men too could now rejoice. Perhaps they too would testify of Christ to their own people. As they made ready to leave, God warned them in a dream not to return to Herod. They obeyed the warning and journeyed to their own country by another way.

In order to protect Jesus, an angel instructed Joseph in a dream: "Arise, and take the young child and his mother, and flee into Egypt, and be thou there until I bring thee word: for Herod will seek the young child to destroy him." The family promptly departed into Egypt. (See Matthew 2:1—14.)

King Herod waited for the return of the wise men. When it became obvious that they had ignored him, he was furious. Calculating the earliest time the baby could have been born, using the time the wise men told him they had first seen the star, he ordered the slaughter of all the children in Bethlehem "and in all the coasts thereof" (Matthew 2:16) who were two years old and younger.

John, the infant son of Zacharias and Elisabeth, apparently lived near Bethlehem with his parents. When Zacharias heard of Herod's order to kill the innocent children, he instructed Elisabeth to take John into the mountains. He knew he must protect his promised son, who must live to prepare the people to receive the Messiah, Jesus Christ. Later, when he refused to tell where his young son was hidden, by Herod's order Zacharias was slain in the temple at Jerusalem. (See Joseph Smith, *Teachings of the Prophet Joseph Smith*, sel. Joseph Fielding Smith, Salt Lake City: Deseret Book Company, 1938, p. 261; hereinafter referred to as *Teachings.*)

Shortly after these murderous acts, and while yet plotting further bloodshed by the mass execution of leading Jews in Jerusalem, Herod died. The joy of the people over his death was short-lived. By order of Rome, Herod's dominion in Palestine was divided, and each of his sons now ruled one third—Philip in the northeast, Antipas in Galilee and Perea, and Archelaus in Judea, Idumea, and Samaria.

When Herod died, Joseph brought Mary and the young child Jesus out of Egypt back to Palestine. On reaching their homeland they learned that Archelaus, Herod's most wicked son, now ruled in Judea. Joseph was warned in a dream and went north into Galilee to find safety and peace.

The family made their home in the city of Nazareth, and here the Savior spent his childhood and youth. He helped Joseph with his work as a carpenter. He studied the law and the scriptures, and he absorbed the beauty of the land in which he lived—the fertile fields of the lower valleys, the meadows outside of the city, and Nazareth itself, with its terraced streets and gardens nestled against the hillside.

When he became twelve, Jesus went with Joseph and Mary to Jerusalem for the feast of the Passover. Having reached that age, he now attended the temple ceremonies as a recognized member of the congregation, and took part with them in the celebration.

A large company of relatives and friends came from Nazareth to Jerusalem. When the feast was over, and the group had already traveled a day's journey back toward Galilee, Joseph and Mary realized that Jesus was missing. Not finding him in the group, they hastily returned to the city.

After three anxious days they found him in the temple. There he had joined in the discussions commonly led by the Jewish religious leaders called doctors or rabbis. As Jesus participated, the discussion changed. The doctors began "hearing him, and asking him questions," and they were "astonished at his understanding, and answers" (JST Luke 2:46—47).

When his mother expressed her and Joseph's great concern at having lost Jesus, he gently replied, "How is it that ye sought me? wist ye not that I must be about my Father's business?" (Luke 2:49). With that statement he bore testimony of his divine Father. He was indeed the Son of God, and he was growing in the understanding that his life's work would not be found with Joseph in the carpenter's shop but in helping his Father "bring to pass the immortality and eternal life of man" (Moses 1:39).

Nevertheless, Jesus was obedient to Joseph and Mary and returned with them to Nazareth. There the normal

family routines were again taken up. Though Mary pondered the unfolding events of Jesus' life, she could not
comprehend them fully. Had his divinity been always
apparent, he would not have been able to experience the
natural conditions of earth life. At birth, he too could not
remember his former life. He was subject to pain and
temptation. He knew sorrow and disappointment. Yet he
learned through his complete obedience, and he grew
from "grace to grace" (D&C 93:13). The central focus of
his life was to do the will of his Father in Heaven. His days
were filled with work, both mental and physical. He keen-
ly observed and understood all that was around him. And
thus he "grew up with his brethren, and waxed strong,
and waited upon the Lord for the time of his ministry to
come" (JST Matthew 3:24).

Chapter 3

PREPARATION FOR HIS MISSION

About thirty years had now passed since the birth of Jesus. John, the long-awaited son of Zacharias and Elisabeth, was six months older than the Savior. While Jesus was living in Nazareth, John was in the desert area in the south of Judea. Each was being prepared for his earthly ministry as foretold by the ancient prophets.

John's prophetic mission was to go before and "make ready a people prepared for the Lord" (Luke 1:17). The Lord's covenant people had wandered far from the teachings of the prophets. There was much wickedness in the land, especially among the rulers and priests in high places. Their concern was for themselves and in the satisfying of their own selfish desires. They dressed luxuriously and held power among their associates. A man of great courage and faith would be needed to reach these people. It would require one who was bold, outspoken, fearless and righteous; one who would stand out from the rest; one who would be as a "voice . . . crying in the wilderness" (Mark 1:3).

John was this man. He had lived apart from others and ate what the desert provided—locusts and wild honey. His garments were of rough cloth made of camel's hair, and he wore a girdle of skin around his waist. His concern was not for himself but for the importance of his message.

John's preparation for his mission began very early in his life. He was filled with the Holy Ghost before he was born. He "was baptized while he was yet in his childhood, and was ordained by the angel of God at the time he was eight days old" (D&C 84:28). He was tutored by divine teachers while living in the wilderness. He held the priesthood, which included "the keys of the ministering of angels" (D&C 13:1), and he experienced the companionship of the Holy Ghost. He was the only one on the face of the earth authorized to carry the message that would prepare the way for the coming of the Lord.

Suddenly the news began to spread throughout all the land of Israel. It was said that a new prophet had come telling the people: "Repent: . . . for the kingdom of heaven is at hand" (Matthew 3:2). From all parts of the land, out of the cities and the villages, the people came. Some walked, some rode their animals, but all moved toward the River Jordan where John was teaching the word of the Lord with authority and power. He taught them the first principles of the gospel. He spoke of faith, repentance, baptism by immersion, and a higher baptism by fire or the bestowal of the Holy Ghost by someone who had more authority than he possessed. He used all of his energies to teach and persuade the people that the kingdom of God was at hand.

Some of the people thrilled with his message. Others resisted, because his teachings made them aware of their sins. Still others hardened their hearts and held to the traditions taught by the rulers. John's message was so powerful that many who were humble and believed desired to repent, to serve God, and to be baptized. The new prophet became known as John the Baptist. He had authority and baptized the people by immersion in the Jordan River, symbolizing that their sins were washed away and that they had entered into a covenant with the Lord.

There was great excitement in the land as the word spread and many were drawn to hear this messenger from God. People began to question and wonder. Could this be the Christ that God promised to send long ago, the Messiah who would rule over his people? When John realized their thoughts, he told them: "I indeed baptize you with water; but one mightier than I" will come, and he will baptize you with "the Holy Ghost and with fire." John did not want the people to worship him. He was sent to prepare them to accept the Savior. Again he explained this by saying, "One mightier than I cometh, the latchet of whose shoes I am not worthy to unloose" (Luke 3:16).

When Jesus was about thirty years of age, he journeyed from his home in Nazareth to the Jordan River. It was time to begin his ministry, and for John, the forerunner-prophet, it was time to meet the Messiah of whom he bore testimony.

As John was teaching on the banks of the Jordan, he looked up and saw Jesus coming toward him from among the multitude. He recognized immediately that this man was different from all others. He was a man without sin. Since baptism was performed for the remission of sins, John felt this man had no need for repentance or baptism. As Jesus approached, John spoke saying that he should not baptize him. He explained, "I have need to be baptized of thee, and comest thou to me?"

Jesus then taught John by explaining that he did need to be baptized. This was not because of sin, but "to fulfil all righteousness" (Matthew 3:14—15). Through being baptized Jesus would receive an ordinance necessary to enter the kingdom of God. He would make a covenant with the Father to obey all his commandments, and through his humility and obedience, he would set the example for all men to follow. (See 2 Nephi 31:4—11.)

The calm waters of the Jordan River with olive trees bending over its banks had been the setting for many miracles in the past. On this eventful day, John took Jesus and baptized him by immersion in the same manner that he had baptized the others. But when Jesus came up out of the water, it was different. John's soul was filled with great joy. The heavens were open, and he saw "the Spirit descending from heaven like a dove," to rest upon Jesus (John 1:32). Then John heard the voice of God the Father: "This is my beloved Son, in whom I am well pleased." This was the Christ he had promised to send. Jesus was his divine Son, and he directed people for all time to "Hear . . . him" (JST Matthew 3:46).

The Savior, realizing the magnitude of his earthly mission, was now prompted to seek solitude in a place where he could be alone, free from any worldly distractions. Thus the Spirit led him "into the wilderness, to be with God." (JST Matthew 4:1). Here he sought spiritual strength and divine guidance from his Father for the greatest task ever to be accomplished in this world. While in the wilderness he chose to fast so that his mortal body would be in complete harmony with the divine influence of his Father's will. Here over a period of forty days, he was instructed and received revelation. (See Bruce R. McConkie, *The Mortal Messiah*, 4 vols., Salt Lake City: Deseret Book Company, 1979-1981, 1:408—10; hereinafter referred to as *The Mortal Messiah*.)

After Jesus had fasted those forty days and forty nights and had "communed with God" (JST Matthew 4:2), he was hungry and physically weak. Satan was well aware of this, and he sought to take advantage of the Savior at this time when he might be least resistant to temptation. He came to Jesus and confronted him. His first evil design was to entice Jesus to satisfy the craving of his mortal body for food. He also struck at the very heart of the relationship which Jesus had with his Father. Taunting Jesus, he said, "If thou be the Son of God, command that these stones be made bread." Prove to me that you are the Son of God. It was a selfish and spectacular misuse of Jesus' divine power that Satan desired.

Jesus' reply to the tempter was clear and unwavering. He did not need to prove what was a fact. He knew the scriptures, the word of God, and replied, "It is written, Man shall not live by bread alone, but by every word that proceedeth out of the mouth of God." Bread might save life physically, but Jesus knew that obedience to the Father's word was the source of life eternally. The Savior was determined to obey his Father.

Although Satan saw the failure of his first attempt to thwart Jesus, he was not about to give up. Jesus was transported by the Spirit into the holy city to the pinnacle of the temple where he could see the spacious courts below.

Here Satan tried his evil designs a second time and challenged: "If thou be the Son of God, cast thyself down: for it is written, He shall give his angels charge concerning thee: . . . they shall bear thee up."

Cleverly, Satan now also quoted scripture, a prophecy telling of the coming Messiah. (See Psalms 91:11–12.) Why not fulfil the prophecy now? Such a dramatic display of power would surely provide public recognition of Jesus' superior being. But Jesus would not yield to the tempter. He knew that his divine powers were not given him to gratify personal desires but to bless those he was sent to serve. His followers would be drawn to him and remain with him by their own choice; and the witness of the Spirit would hold them, not the spectacle of miracles. In response to Satan, Jesus countered from the scriptures, "It is written, . . . Thou shalt not tempt the Lord thy God."

Satan's wicked onslaught was not over. On a high mountain he confronted the Savior a third time. Jesus was shown the wealth of nations, of cities and fields and flocks and herds. He saw the power of kings and kingdoms and the glories of all the earth. Then Satan said to Jesus, "All these things will I give thee, if thou wilt fall down and worship me."

Satan struck at the weakness of many who experience mortality—the desire for wealth and the desire for influence and power over others. But in the eternal perspective, his offer was not only evil but foolish. Jesus knew that in being faithful and obedient to his Father's commandments he would inherit "all that [the] Father hath" (D&C 84:38), and so would every other obedient son or daughter of God. Though Jesus had his agency and was capable of sinning and could have succumbed to the temptations of Satan, he did not yield. Wisely, he would not accommodate or listen to the tempter further. With dignity and unwavering control, he now commanded: "Get thee hence, Satan: for it is written, Thou shalt worship the Lord thy God, and him only shalt thou serve." (See JST Matthew 4:2—5; Matthew 4:3—10.)

Satan departed in anger and defeat. He had given up his unsuccessful temptations for a season.

Jesus was unwavering in his determination to carry out his mission. But although he was the Son of God and was without sin, yet he learned obedience "by the things which he suffered" (Hebrews 5:8). He had the power to alleviate any discomfort, but he suffered "temptations of every kind" (Alma 7:11) and "pain of body, hunger, thirst, and fatigue" (Mosiah 3:7). In so doing, he gained the understanding necessary to help and nurture his people, and he gained the strength to prove his absolute loyalty to his Father and his earthly mission.

After this confrontation with Satan, Jesus was ready for his mission. He had been baptized, had been instructed and received revelation from his Father, and had not yielded to the temptations of the adversary. The Savior of the world was ready now to leave the great solitude of the wilderness and return to the people he would serve and love, heal and teach, as he went about his earthly ministry.

Chapter 4

HOW TO ENTER THE KINGDOM OF GOD

During the time that Jesus was in the wilderness, John continued to cry repentance and to baptize those with worthy desires. Talk of this new prophet and his message had become so widespread that in Jerusalem the religious leaders became curious and very concerned. Who was this man who was drawing so many people to him and threatening their position? They personally dared not give any hint of recognition to this new teacher, so they appointed a delegation of priests and Levites from among the Pharisees. They were directed to go to John and inquire about his identity and authority.

When this group arrived at the Jordan and began to question John, he responded with directness: "I am not the Christ." He further explained that he was not any of the other individuals they might have supposed him to be. Because the approval of their leaders in this assignment was undoubtedly very important to them, the delegation now asked John, "Who art thou? that we may give an answer to them that sent us."

John was anxious to teach these men. He told them of his calling and why he was baptizing. He quoted the scriptures to them and declared that he was, as foretold by Isaiah the prophet, the one who would call the people to repentance to prepare for the coming of the Lord. The official delegation resisted being told to repent and immediately demanded of him his authority for baptizing. John now stood fearlessly before these representatives from the Pharisaic party and bore his testimony. He did not heed the fact that he appeared different in his rough clothing. He was not threatened or intimidated because he was not recognized as one having authority from those in high places. With courage and conviction, he told these men that the Redeemer of the world was among them and that they did not know him. He would verify his authority. The officials listened intently and with great concern as they anticipated carrying this report back to their self-serving leaders. (See John 1:20-28.)

John had answered the immediate questions that satisfied the delegation, and he fearlessly continued his mission. On the following day, as the Savior returned to Bethabara by the Jordan River to begin his ministry, John openly declared to his followers and all the world: "Behold the Lamb of God, which taketh away the sin of the world." For hundreds of years the Jews and all the Israelites before them had offered sacrifices as a way of looking forward to the atonement to be made by the Son of God. Surely those who were aware of the spiritual meaning of these sacrifices must have thrilled at John's witness that the Lamb of God was now among them.

John spoke by the power and authority of a prophet. With great intensity he told of the sign given him at Jesus' baptism. "I saw the Spirit descending from heaven like a dove, and it abode upon him.

"And I knew him not: but he that sent me to baptize with water . . . said unto me, Upon whom thou shalt see the Spirit descending, and remaining on him, the same is he which baptizeth with the Holy Ghost." After this explanation, John fervently testified, "I saw, and bare record that this is the Son of God." (See John 1:29—34.)

The next morning, as John continued to teach the people, two young men listened intently. They were fishermen and had come all the way from the Sea of Galilee to hear his message. One was named Andrew and the other John.

As they listened to John the Baptist, Jesus walked nearby. John taught them, again declaring, "Behold the Lamb of God." John desired his followers to be led to Christ.

Andrew and John were so impressed by John's testimony that they immediately wanted to be near and hear Jesus. When the Savior saw that they were following him, he asked in a gentle, courteous way what it was they wanted. They replied that they would like to know where he was staying so they could talk with him. "Come and see" was his reassuring invitation. The two young men joyously went with Jesus, and he taught them all the rest of that day. The experiences of those hours filled their souls with happiness and wonder and the spirit of testimony. (See John 1:35—39.)

Andrew and John each had a brother they were eager to have know Jesus. Andrew's brother was named Simon, and John's brother was named James. All four of these young men were fishermen from Galilee.

Andrew found his brother first and was eager to tell him the startling news, "We have found . . . the Christ." He wanted him to see and hear and feel what he had felt. When Jesus saw Andrew and his brother, Simon, coming toward him, without waiting to hear his name, he said, "Thou art Simon the son of Jona: thou shalt be called Cephas." The Lord honored Simon by giving him this new name. Cephas is translated Peter and means rock. From this time on Simon was called Simon Peter. (See John 1:41—42.)

Andrew, John, and Simon Peter became Jesus' followers. The next day, Jesus travelled to Galilee. On the way he met Philip and his friend Nathanael. As Jesus found these men who had been chosen in the premortal existence to be his special witnesses, he recognized them and called them to follow, and they came and walked with him. (See *Jesus the Christ*, p. 141.)

This little company of Jesus' first disciples were invited to a wedding in a small town near Nazareth called Cana. Jesus' mother was there and apparently had some responsibility for the guests. After the celebration continued for some time, she came to him and explained that there was a shortage of wine.

Jesus knew his divine power was only to be used at properly appointed times. On this occasion he instructed the servants to fill the six large stone water pots nearby with water. They filled them to the brim. Later as the servants drew from the pots, they saw that it was no longer water but wine. Without any public display, Jesus had caused the water to be turned to wine. It was a miracle. It demonstrated to his disciples his divine power over physical matter. It caused them to wonder and ponder and to strengthen their faith. (See John 2:1—11.)

Following the wedding celebration, Jesus, with his

mother and disciples, traveled to Capernaum which lies on the north shore of the Sea of Galilee. In this area Jesus would eventually spend most of his time. It was one of many cities in a district around the lake that was very fertile and known for its beauty.

Jesus did not stay long in Capernaum. The feast of the Passover was approaching, and every faithful Israelite would turn his thoughts to Jerusalem and the holy temple. The law required that all male Jews attend the celebration, make the necessary offerings at the temple, and observe the paschal feast. All this was done to remind the people of the Lord's goodness to Israel, of his saving them from death and delivering them from Egypt.

Jesus now made his way to Jerusalem. It had been eighteen years since he, as a boy of twelve, had answered the questions of the rabbis in the temple. Now he had begun his ministry and was again on his way there to be about his Father's business.

No doubt many people were watching Jesus as he walked through the streets toward the temple, his Father's house. Many of the people in Jerusalem had heard of John's testimony that Jesus was the Son of God. People had reason to wonder what he might do when he saw what was taking place. The streets were filled with the shouting of merchants selling their wares—the items needed for the celebration. People were being forced to pay high prices to buy animals and birds to offer as a sacrifice.

As Jesus entered the outer courtyard of the temple, the stench of animals and filth hung in the air. Stalls of oxen and pens filled with sheep crowded the courtyard. Cages of birds lined the walls. The noise of the animals was mingled with the shouts of their owners extolling their merits and with the rising voices of the money changers who were at their tables gathering enormous profits. (See *Jesus the Christ,* pp. 167-68.)

Jesus would not tolerate this desecration of his Father's house. Quickly he made a whip of small cords, and with righteous anger and great strength he drove the sheep and oxen and their merchants out of the temple. With force he overturned the money changers' tables and sent their coins scattering into the litter and dung on the floor. He ordered those selling doves to take their cages away. With authority he declared, "Make not my Father's house an house of merchandise" (John 2:16).

After this public display in defense of the holy temple no one stepped forward to demand his arrest, not even those religious leaders who regulated the temple. They did not call their temple guard. They did not call the Roman soldiers. Their misuse and desecration of God's house was so apparent to them and the public, and their guilt so strong, that they could not protest. Afterward, they only weakly inquired as to why Jesus had felt it was his responsibility to cleanse the temple. "Show us a sign," they said. They wanted him to demonstrate his authority. Even this request indicated their concern for the possibility that this man from Galilee might be the Messiah as his disciples claimed. Jesus had little respect for these men and their request for a sign, but he answered them saying, "Destroy this temple, and in three days I will raise it up" (John 2:19).

The Jews answered with great pride that it had taken forty-six years to build their temple. Indignant, they asked how he would build such a structure in three days!

Jesus was not speaking of the temple on Mount Moriah. He was speaking of his own body as a temple. He was referring to his future death and resurrection. Though the Jews pretended not to understand, they would not forget this incident or what Jesus had said.

Jesus became the most talked-about person at this Passover. His ministry was now a matter of great interest to everyone. His presence in Jerusalem and his teachings had divided the people. The Jewish rulers, threatened by his power and authority, began a deadly rivalry with Jesus. Yet others flocked to his side. These people were drawn to him because of his teachings and miracles, but it was probably more because of Jesus' acts at the Passover festival that the people would not forget who he was.

Among the Jewish leaders in Jerusalem was a man named Nicodemus. He was a Pharisee and a member of the great Sanhedrin, the ruling council. During the nighttime he made his way through the narrow streets of Jerusalem to a home where Jesus was staying. He wanted to talk with the Savior privately under the cover of darkness. Undoubtedly he was afraid to be seen by his associates. Yet he overcame his fears and prejudice, for he was driven by a desire to know more. Jesus would not turn him away because of the lateness of the hour or because he was a Pharisee.

As their conversation began, Nicodemus recognized that Jesus was more than a great teacher, for he said, "No man can do these miracles that thou doest, except God be with him." During the quiet of that night, Jesus personally taught this Jewish leader the first principles of the gospel. He began: "Verily, verily, I say unto thee, Except a man be born again, he cannot see the kingdom of God."

Nicodemus was confused. How could a man that had been born once be born again? Jesus patiently continued. He wanted Nicodemus to understand that a man must have faith in him, Jesus Christ, as the Son of God, must repent and turn away from sin, and must have a new birth through baptism. He must be "born of water and of the Spirit" if he is to enter the kingdom of heaven. To be born of the water is to be baptized by immersion for the remission of sins by one having authority from God. To be born of the Spirit is to experience through obedience and faithfulness the cleansing power of the Atonement and to receive guidance and direction from the Holy Ghost. Such a person begins a new life—a life filled with purpose—as he becomes alive to the things of the Spirit. (See Moses 6:59—60, 62; Mosiah 18:8—10; Alma 7:15—16.)

Jesus then reminded Nicodemus of the witness of Moses to the children of Israel about their future Savior. He explained God's plan and infinite love for his children: "For God so loved the world, that he gave his only begotten Son, that whosoever believeth in him should not perish, but have everlasting life."

Nicodemus listened. He asked questions and was taught. He perhaps came very near to accepting Christ at this time, yet he left with the burden of choice still upon him. His steps took him back to his daily walk and his position with his associates of the Sanhedrin. But having once been taught by the Master, could he ever return wholly to what he was? (See John 3:1—21.)

In the following months Jesus taught and baptized throughout Judea. John also continued his ministry, calling the people to repentance. He baptized them and told them to follow Christ. He knew he must direct his disciples to walk with the Master.

Though John realized his work was drawing to a close, he continued courageously. He spoke out against Herod Antipas, the ruler appointed by the Romans over

the province of Galilee and Perea. Herod Antipas was as
wicked as his father who had ordered the death of the children in Bethlehem. Antipas was by an illegal marriage to
Herodias openly living in adultery, and John, who had
been sent to cry repentance, accused and confronted him
with his sins: "It is not lawful for thee to have thy brother's wife" (Mark 6:18).

Herod reacted swiftly. He wanted to have John
killed, but because the people considered John a prophet,
he dared not. Instead, he had John imprisoned at
Machaerus, a fortress on the northeastern shore of the
Dead Sea.

Jesus knew that John, who had so fearlessly carried
out his commission to be his forerunner, now suffered persecution and imprisonment. His heart must have ached for
his beloved disciple, but he must continue in the mission
for which John had prepared the way. Because of his great
love for John, through his divine power, Jesus "sent
angels, and, behold, they came and ministered unto him."
(JST Matthew 4:11.) John was not left alone.

Chapter 5

"THY FAITH HATH MADE THEE WHOLE"

The Savior left the area around Jerusalem intending to go north to Galilee. But he told his disciples that they would travel by the direct route—through Samaria. This must have startled them, for Jewish travelers considered this route unsafe. The Samaritans were descendants of Jews who had intermarried with other nations. Because of their mixed heritage there was an intense hatred between the Samaritans and the Jews, and this area was often the scene of bloodshed and violence.

From northern Judea, where Jesus had been teaching and baptizing, over the mountain to Sychar, a little village in Samaria, was a distance of some twenty miles along a rugged and hilly road. The Savior arrived at Jacob's Well near the village thirsty and hungry from the long journey. Many hundreds of years earlier this well had belonged to Jacob, the ancestor of the Israelites. He had given it with a parcel of ground to his son Joseph. It was still known as Jacob's Well.

While his disciples went into the village to buy food,
Jesus purposely remained behind, resting for a time by
the well. He had within himself the power to provide
food and drink for his relief, but in all things he chose to
subject himself to the experiences of mortal life. (See
Bruce R. McConkie, *Doctrinal New Testament Commentary*, 3 vols., Salt Lake City: Bookcraft, 1970-1973,
p. 151; hereinafter referred to as *Commentary*.)

A woman of Samaria came to the well in her long,
flowing clothes as she regularly did to fill her water jug.
As she approached, she saw Jesus sitting on the stone
wall by the well. The woman must have been very surprised when he spoke to her, a woman he did not know,
especially a Samaritan woman. He asked her for a drink
of water. Ordinarily, a request for a drink to quench
thirst and save life would be readily given, and yet she
hesitated. She wondered why a Jew would ask a favor of
a Samaritan, however great the need. She inquired,
"How is it that thou, being a Jew, askest drink of me,
which am a woman of Samaria? for the Jews have no
dealings with the Samaritans."

Jesus again introduced a great truth to a single
individual. "If thou knewest . . . who it is that saith to
thee, Give me to drink; thou wouldst have asked of him,
and he would have given thee living water," he said. The
woman, seeing that he had no container with which to
draw from the well, was bewildered. Jesus wanted her to
understand. He explained to her that the water she drew
from the well was only of temporary benefit. She would
always have to return to the well again and again to re-
lieve her thirst and sustain life. Then he taught her:
"Whosoever drinketh of the water that I shall give him
shall never thirst; but the water that I shall give him shall

be in him a well of water springing up into everlasting life." The "living water" which Jesus offered was the true understanding of God, his own forthcoming atonement, and the teachings of the gospel that would bring salvation.

The woman of Samaria was puzzled. She did not know who Jesus was. Now he reached out to help her understand. He asked her to go and call her husband and return. She told Jesus that she had no husband. Jesus let her know of his divine power by telling her that she had spoken the truth, that the man she was living with was not her husband, and that she had had five husbands before him.

Hearing this truth from a stranger caused her to confess saying, "Sir, I perceive that thou art a prophet." Amazed at his knowledge of her personal life, she explained to Jesus her belief that when Christ would come he would be able to know all things. To her great amazement Jesus said, "I that speak unto thee am he."

This woman in sin to whom the Christ himself had offered "living water" left her water jar at the well and hurried into the city to tell her friends. Earnestly she implored them: "Come, see a man, which told me all things that ever I did: is not this the Christ?" A crowd of Samaritans then followed her out from the city. Some probably came out of curiosity and others on the strength of the woman's testimony. When these people of Samaria, who were so despised by others, felt the love Jesus had for them, they asked that he stay with them. Graciously, he accepted their invitation to remain.

After the people heard Jesus themselves, many believed and said to the woman who was taught at the well: "Now we believe, not because of thy saying: for we have

heard him ourselves, and know that this is indeed the
Christ, the Saviour of the world." They had gained a
testimony of their own. (See John 4:9—30, 39—42.)

After spending two days with the Samaritans, Jesus
continued on his journey to Galilee. This was his homeland where as a youth he had roamed the rugged hill areas
and enjoyed the sunny meadows and open fields. He
loved Galilee. When he reached the city of Cana, a
nobleman pleaded humbly for Jesus to heal his son, who
was near death. He had come all the way from Capernaum to ask in faith that his son's life be spared. Jesus
spoke the words of relief, "Thy son liveth" (John 4:51).
The nobleman returned home and found his great faith in
Jesus fulfilled. His son had been healed.

Jesus made his way to Nazareth to teach among the
people he loved and had grown up with. He wanted to tell
them of the gospel. He went to the synagogue where he
had worshipped as a boy, but on this Sabbath day he now
attended as a recognized teacher of legal age. At the
appropriate point in the service, he stood up to read and
was handed the book of Isaiah. Jesus read from what in
our Bible is the sixty-first chapter the prophecies about the
promised Messiah. As he finished reading and took his
seat, which was customary before beginning the discussion, his first statement was astonishing—especially to
those who remembered him only as the carpenter's son
and had watched him grow up as a boy in their community. His testimony was forthright and direct. "This day is
this scripture fulfilled in your ears," he said (Luke 4:21).
Thus he told them that he was the long-awaited Messiah
of whom Isaiah had written.

Many in the congregation wondered at his words,
saying, "Is not this Joseph's son?" (Luke 4:22). Jesus knew
the thoughts in their hearts. They wanted a sign, a mira-

cle. They knew of the miracle in Cana and of the boy in Capernaum who had been healed and of the things Jesus did when he was in Jerusalem. Jesus graciously spoke to his townspeople and gave examples of miracles from the Old Testament, explaining that they happened only when the people had the necessary faith.

The people were offended. As far as they were concerned, Jesus was only the son of the village carpenter. For him to suggest that they lacked faith and were classed with the unbelievers put them in a violent rage. Angered by his testimony, they rose up against him. They took him out of the city and were determined to cast him off the rocky cliffs of Nazareth. But Jesus, with power from God, stepped away from the mob unharmed. (See Luke 4:16–30.)

The Savior left Nazareth with a heavy heart. Because of their lack of faith, he was not able to bring the gospel message to the people he loved and had grown up with. Nazareth would no longer be his home.

Sometime after this, Jesus returned to the Sea of Galilee. It was not a large sea, but, shaped like a great heart, its waters had been a source of life to millions over the ages. At times its surface was rough and wind-driven, and at others it was calm and serene. Countless fish from this sea fed thousands of people. Here Simon Peter and his brother Andrew, and James and John and their father Zebedee made their living as fishermen.

As Jesus walked along the shore, he called these men into a closer association with him. He knew them, and he knew what they were to become.

Crowds of people had gathered around the Savior anxious to hear one who taught with power and authority. Jesus stepped into Peter's ship and asked him to move it out from the shore where the people might possibly see and hear him better. Jesus sat down and taught the people out of the ship. After he finished his message to them, he asked Peter to go further out into the deep water and let down his nets for fish. Peter explained that they had been fishing all night and caught nothing, but with some hesitation he finally agreed to do what the Master asked.

When Peter let down his nets and followed the instructions given by Jesus, such a great number of fish filled the nets that they broke. He quickly called for help to his partners, James and John, who were in a second ship close by. When the net was gathered, both ships were filled with so many fish that they almost sank. The disciples were overwhelmed and astonished. Jesus had already called these men to follow him and to become fishers of men. After this experience, he reminded them again, "From henceforth thou shalt catch men." (See Luke 5:1–10.)

After this experience, these young men, "believing on his words" (JST Matthew 4:19), left their work, their fishing, the mending of their nets, the employment of their father (in the case of James and John), "and when they had brought their ships to land, they forsook all, and followed him" (Luke 5:11).

One Sabbath day in Capernaum was a great day of miracles. Jesus began the day in the synagogue and there cast out an evil spirit from a man, thereby causing the people to marvel at his power and authority. Jesus then went to Simon Peter's house. There he found Peter's mother-in-law sick with a burning fever. The family asked for his help, and Jesus with loving compassion "touched her hand, and the fever left her" (Matthew 8:15). She then arose and extended her hospitality to Jesus and those who were with him.

All during that day and on into the evening after

sunset, people flocked to Jesus. They brought their friends and relatives to hear him and to be healed. The Savior did what no one else could do. He healed those with sick bodies as well as those with sick souls. Jesus "laid his hands on every one of them" and healed all those who "believed on his name" (Luke 4:40; JST Matthew 4:22).

The next morning after this great day of teaching and healing and the miracle at Peter's house, Jesus arose before daybreak and went out to a place where he could be alone and pray to his Father. He wanted always to do his Father's will, and he prayed for direction and renewed strength for his work.

Soon Peter and the other disciples missed Jesus. They went looking for him, and when they found him they told him that everyone was looking for him and asking that he return. The people of Capernaum did not want Jesus to leave. But Jesus kindly explained to these eager followers that he could not remain longer with them for he must "preach the kingdom of God to other cities also" (Luke 4:43).

Jesus now went throughout all of Galilee preaching to the people in the synagogues, healing the sick, and casting out devils. The Savior, who had suffered pains and afflictions and temptations of every kind, took upon himself the pains and the sickness of his people. (See Alma 7:11–12.) Having experienced their infirmities himself, he was filled with great love and compassion and mercy and knew how to care for them according to their needs. Even the lepers, who were filled with a disease that rotted away their flesh, felt the touch of his healing hands. (See Matthew 8:1–3.)

When Jesus returned again to Capernaum, word spread rapidly that he was there. The people knew where he was staying, and they came from all over Galilee and

Judea and even from Jerusalem. So great was the crowd that even the doorways of the house were filled and late-comers could not get near the Master. To all that were within hearing distance, Jesus preached the gospel.

At the edge of this great crowd came a party of four carrying on a couch a man who was afflicted with palsy, a disease that made his limbs shake constantly. The man was helpless to even form the words to express his needs. Yet his friends had such great faith and were so desirous that he be healed that they had carried him all the way to where Jesus was staying. Now they saw the great number of people around the house. But they were not discouraged. Perhaps there was an outside stairway, or they used a ladder. Carefully, they lifted their friend on his couch up to the flat roof of the house. To the surprise of the crowd, they broke away part of the roof and gently lowered in front of Jesus the couch on which the man lay.

Jesus was deeply touched by the faith of those who had labored so hard to place their friend before him. Looking into the eyes of the sufferer, he knew of his trusting faith. In the midst of the onlookers and with great compassion, Jesus said, "Thy sins are forgiven thee" (Luke 5:20). Jesus told him to arise from his bed and go home. The man arose. He was healed. Carrying the mattress on which he had been lying, he walked out before them.

People were utterly amazed and wondered at the things they had seen that day. Among the crowd were also enemies of Jesus, scribes and Pharisees, who now hated him even more because—not being God (in their eyes)—he had said that which only God could properly say: "Your sins are forgiven," and because they saw how the people believed in him and praised God for sending him.

When Jesus arrived in Jerusalem to celebrate the feast of the Passover a second time, he had been teaching among the people for over a year. The proud Jewish religious leaders knew of his miracles in Galilee, and they were envious and angered by his works. When they heard how the Savior had just healed a lame man on the Sabbath day at the pool of Bethesda near the temple, they tried to discredit him and accuse him of breaking the laws of the Sabbath. But when they confronted Jesus, from the scriptures he taught them of his divinity. He urged these men, who were honored in their lofty positions as scholars and to whom the people looked as the interpreters of the word of God, to "search the scriptures," for they "testify of me" (John 5:39).

How these men resisted being corrected and taught by Jesus! They began thereafter to spy on his actions and plot to destroy him. The Savior, realizing their intent and wanting to reach as many people as possible with his message, returned to the relative peace of Galilee.

As great multitudes followed Jesus, he knew that the time had come when others must be called and given the power and authority which he had to teach and bless and heal, that more and more people might receive the gospel message.

In the evening, Jesus went alone into a mountain not far from Capernaum to pray. All through the night he prayed to God his Father. He had a very important matter to talk with him about. "And when it was day, he called unto him his disciples: and of them he chose twelve, whom also he named apostles." Apostle means "one who is sent." Of those who followed him, Jesus ordained twelve men to this "office and calling belonging to the Higher or Melchizedek Priesthood." (See *Jesus the Christ*, pp. 227—28.) They would become his special witnesses. The men chosen according to the will of God for this sacred trust were: Simon Peter; Andrew, his brother; James and John; Philip and Nathanael (also called Bartholemew); Matthew and Thomas; James the son of Alphaeus; Simon Zelotes; Judas the brother of James; and Judas Iscariot, who acted as the treasurer for the Twelve. (See Luke 6:12—16.)

Following their ordination, Jesus wanted to prepare the Apostles to teach and administer in the authority of the office which they now held. He took them, with many of his faithful disciples, up into a mountain to give special instruction to the Twelve and to teach them and the disciples of their responsibilities as members of the Church. There he lovingly taught them that for those who were the poor in spirit, who had lost their loved ones in death, who were meek, who hungered to become righteous, who were merciful and pure in heart, who were peacemakers, and even who were persecuted for his sake—for all such, great blessings lay in store. They would inherit the kingdom of heaven. They would be comforted with peace that surpassed all understanding. They would inherit the earth and be filled with the Holy Ghost. They would obtain mercy. They would see God and be called his children. All these promises and blessings and the description of the Christlike attributes man could attain were called the Beatitudes, and all were based on their acceptance of him and obedience to the principles of his gospel. (See Matthew 5:1-12.)

Jesus then spoke to them about the obligation of being a disciple. He likened them to the light of the world and told them to let their light shine so others would see their good works and be led to their Father in Heaven.

(See Matthew 5:14—16.) He spoke of the law of Moses and introduced them to a higher law, the gospel of Christ. On this mountain overlooking the area around about, and away from the multitudes who were now following him everywhere, Jesus spoke to this select group and taught them principles of righteousness. Having been instructed by the Master himself, they were now responsible to live and teach his gospel—a gospel that would change the hearts of men and bring them lasting joy.

Jesus returned to Capernaum and tirelessly continued to respond to the needs of his followers. He taught and demonstrated to the Apostles the power of the priesthood which they now held. He healed the servant of an officer in the Roman army. He did it without even being in the presence of one who was ill. (See Matthew 8:5—13.) In the city of Nain, he restored a widow's dead son to life. (See Luke 7:11—15.)

In southern Galilee, Simon, one of the Pharisees, the group who felt themselves so distinctly different from and superior to the common people, invited the Master to dinner. Jesus willingly accepted Simon's invitation, because he had unconditional love for all people and desired to teach them.

It was the custom of the time to receive important guests into one's home with a kiss of welcome and to provide water to wash the dust from their feet, since they wore no shoes or stockings but only sandals. Oil was used for anointing the hair and beard. None of these kindnesses which were due distinguished guests were provided for Jesus in Simon's home. The Savior took his place, probably on one of the low couches, partly sitting and partly reclining while he ate, placing his feet outward from the table.

At that time in Palestine, visitors—even strangers—would enter the house at mealtime and often speak to the guests. A woman came into Simon's house while Jesus was there. She had sinned, and was known for her sin. She bore the scorn of those who professed to be more righteous. But she came seeking the Master, and seeing him, she humbly approached him from behind. Then she bent down to kiss his feet in reverence and gratitude. She may have been one who had so recently heard his words and felt his great compassion as he spoke to the people: "Come unto me, all ye that labour and are heavy laden, and I will give you rest" (Matthew 11:28). The sound of his voice, the power and hope of his message, and the kindness and love of his heart had brought about her conversion. She was now free from the guilt and fear and pain of her past life. (See *The Mortal Messiah*, 2:200.)

This woman kissed the feet of the Savior and in a spirit of sincere gratitude bathed them with her tears. She seemed unaware or unconcerned that disapproving eyes were watching her. With her head bowed reverently, she wiped the Savior's feet with her hair. She had brought an alabaster box of ointment more precious than oil and now anointed his feet. In her heart she knew that Jesus loved and accepted her. Her spirit had found peace and relief.

Jesus graciously permitted her to perform her humble service. Simon watched the great devotion from this woman of the world and thought within himself, though he did not say it, "This man, if he were a prophet, would have known who and what manner of woman this is that touched him: for she is a sinner."

Jesus knew Simon's thoughts and he said, "Simon, I have somewhat to say unto thee."

Simon replied, "Master, say on."

Jesus explained, "There was a certain creditor which had two debtors: the one owed five hundred pence, and the other fifty. And when they had nothing to pay, he frankly forgave them both. Tell me therefore, which of them will love him most?"

Simon must have been feeling quite uncomfortable. "I suppose," he ventured, "that he, to whom he forgave most."

Jesus said, "Thou hast rightly judged." Then he continued, "Seest thou this woman? I entered into thine house, thou gavest me no water for my feet: but she hath washed my feet with tears, and wiped them with the hairs of her head. Thou gavest me no kiss: but this woman since the time I came in hath not ceased to kiss my feet. My head with oil thou didst not anoint: but this woman hath anointed my feet with ointment."

This comparison of Simon's services and heart with that of the woman whom Simon thought a sinner must have been extremely distressful to him. Jesus continued, "I say unto thee, Her sins, which are many, are forgiven; for she loved much: but to whom little is forgiven, the same loveth little."

Jesus now turned to the woman. Through faith and repentance and obedience to the laws of his gospel, the woman had gained forgiveness for her sins. She knew the source of her forgiveness and had come with the precious ointment to express her love to the Savior. Jesus reassured her again that her past sins were no longer to be a burden to her. "Thy sins are forgiven. . . . Go in peace." (See Luke 7:36–50.)

Chapter 6

JESUS' FOLLOWERS MAKE A CHOICE

Though growing multitudes of people were being drawn to Jesus to hear him teach and to be healed both physically and spiritually, others were also gathering strength—those who were opposed to the Savior and his message. There were in the crowds that followed him not only those who came seeking his truth but many who had hardened their hearts and were openly antagonistic.

Jesus was the greatest of teachers. He knew his message, and he knew his followers. Instead of a direct exposition of his doctrine, he began to speak to the people in parables. These simple stories using familiar surroundings and examples to illustrate great messages of truth could be understood only according to the degree of faith in the listener. Jesus said to his disciples, "It is given unto you to know the mysteries of the kingdom of heaven" (Matthew 13:11), because with faith and contemplation and prayer they sought to understand. These were enlightened by the Spirit and were coming to an understanding of the doctrine. To others the truths taught in the parables remained a mystery, because they would not exert themselves or try to understand. Having eyes they did not see, and having ears they did not hear. Many did not wish to be taught "because their hearts were full of iniquity" (*Teachings*, p. 96). Jesus spoke with appreciation for his faithful and chosen followers as he reassured them, "Blessed are your eyes, for they see: and your ears, for they hear" (Matthew 13:16).

Again at the seaside a great multitude gathered from every city to hear his message. He used a fishing boat near by to push out from the shore, and sitting in the boat, he spoke to the multitude who stood waiting. He began with a parable, saying that a sower went out to sow his seed. Some of the seeds fell by the roadside where the ground was hard. Some of the seeds were trodden down, and others were picked up and eaten by the birds. Some of the seeds fell where there were many rocks and not much soil. These seeds grew up quickly, but when the hot sun came they withered and died because their roots were shallow and they could not get moisture. Other seeds could not grow because they fell among briars and thorns that choked them out. Some seeds fell into good soil. They grew and brought forth fruit, some thirty times as much as was sown, some sixty times, and others even a hundred times as much.

Jesus went with his disciples into a house, and there they asked him why he spoke to the people in parables and what the parable about the man sowing his seeds meant. He took time to answer their questions. As they were gathered around him, he helped them understand the hidden message meant only for those who were faithfully seeking light and knowledge.

He explained to them that the sower is the one who

speaks the word of God and the seed is the word of God which he speaks—the gospel message. The field is the world, and the soils are the hearts of those who hear. The seeds by the roadside represent those who hear the gospel but are disobedient and lose their way because the evil one takes away the truth. The seeds in the stony places are those who hear and receive the gospel joyously at first, but because they do not develop deep testimonies for themselves, when tribulation or persecution comes, they fall away. The seeds sown among thorns are those who hear but let the enjoyments of the world crowd the gospel out of their lives, and so it does them little good. Seeds sown in good ground represent those who receive the word of God and are obedient. Their lives produce fruit and abundant goodness. (See Mark 4:1—20; *Jesus the Christ,* pp. 283—84.)

The Savior continued teaching his disciples in the house, hour after hour. He told them the kingdom of heaven is like a treasure which a man found hidden in a field. The man recognized its great value and sold all that he had to buy the field where the treasure was.

He told them the kingdom of heaven is like a merchant who was seeking precious pearls, and when he found the pearl of great price, he sold everything he had to buy the pearl.

Again he explained that the kingdom of heaven is like a net that was cast into the sea and gathered fish of every kind. When it was full, the good fish were kept safely, and the bad were discarded. He likened this parable to the end of the world, when angels would come and the wicked would be separated from the obedient and receive the penalty of their evil acts. (See Matthew 13:44—50.)

When Jesus finished these parables, he asked his disciples if they understood what he had taught them. They said they did. He wanted them to understand his truth just as soon as they were ready to receive it, but he was patient in giving them only as much as they could understand.

Near the close of the day, after Jesus had taught the multitude by the sea and then his disciples in the house, more people continued to gather. He must have needed rest after these many hours of teaching. As they walked down to the shore, he said to his disciples, "Let us pass over unto the other side" (Mark 4:35).

They made the boat ready and moved away from the shore and the crowds. Jesus went to the back of the ship and quickly fell asleep. He was much fatigued, and even though a great storm arose, still he slept on.

The storm increased, and the strong wind made it nearly impossible to manage the boat. The waves broke over the sides. The disciples were terrified, yet Jesus slept on peacefully. Finally, in desperation his disciples cried out, "Master, carest thou not that we perish?" They pleaded with him to save them.

He arose, and in the midst of the fearsome storm and dark night, he sent his voice into the roaring tempest as he rebuked the wind and said to the sea, "Peace, be still." The wind stopped, and there was a great calm. It was quiet as he turned to his disciples and gently but reprovingly asked, "Why are ye so fearful?"

They felt relief and gratitude, but in tones of amazement they asked one another, "What manner of man is this, that even the wind and the sea obey him?" They had witnessed his undeniable power over the forces of nature; even the elements obeyed the Master's will. (See Mark 4:35–41.)

After traveling through the dark and the storm, the small party reached the eastern side of the lake known as the country of the Gadarenes. The disciples must have still been marvelling at the manifestation of Jesus' great power when a man filled with evil spirits came toward them. He was fierce and violent. He lived on the mountain and in the tombs among the dead, and he had been cutting himself with stones. He was a terrifying sight. He had been chained but had broken the chains. No one dared pass by him, for evil spirits possessed his body.

When Jesus saw this tormented man, he spoke to the evil spirit in him: "Come out of the man, thou unclean spirit." The evil spirit in the man cried out, "What have I to do with thee, Jesus, thou Son of the most high God?" These evil spirits recognized the Master.

Jesus said to the evil one, "What is thy name?" And he answered, "My name is Legion: for we are many." A legion was the term given to the major subdivision of an army, so this man was filled with evil spirits. In their wretched plight and in their eagerness to have bodies, they begged that if they must leave the man, they might be allowed to enter the bodies of a herd of swine feeding on the mountainside. Jesus gave permission. The evil spirits went out of the man and entered into the swine. There were about two thousand of them, and suddenly the whole herd ran violently down a steep place into the sea and were drowned.

The men who took care of the swine ran into the city near by and told all the people what had happened to the animals and how the possessed man had been healed. People came in crowds to see for themselves. Amazed, they saw the man who had been filled with evil spirits now clothed and in his right mind and sitting reverently at the feet of the Master.

They were fearful of one who had such power. They were more concerned for the safety of the swine than the healing and teaching of the Savior. Aware of their own sinful ways and having no desire to change, they begged Jesus to leave their country.

The Savior and his disciples returned to the boat and made ready to depart. The man who had been healed was uncertain. He felt such great love and gratitude for the Savior that he pleaded with Jesus that he might go with him. But Jesus forbade him saying, "Go home to thy friends, and tell them how great things the Lord hath done for thee." Reassured and redirected by the Savior, this man became a missionary. He went to his own home town and throughout the area of ten cities, telling people of the marvelous change that Jesus had brought into his life. (See Mark 5:1—20; *Jesus the Christ*, pp. 310—12.)

When Jesus and his disciples recrossed the lake and landed near Capernaum, a large crowd of people was waiting for them there. A man by the name of Jairus, who was one of the rulers of the local synagogue, approached Jesus. Reverently, he fell at his feet and pleaded for the life of his only daughter who had already been near death when he had left his house to find the Savior. "My little daughter lieth at the point of death: I pray thee, come and lay thy hands on her, that she may be healed" (Mark 5:23).

Jesus was tireless in his willingness to respond to those in need. He consented to go with the anxious father to where his little girl was. The disciples accompanied him, and many people followed.

In the crowd that gathered as they walked was another person who needed help. She was a woman who had been ill for many years with an ailment through which she continually lost blood. She had heard of Jesus and knew of his power to heal. She had gone to many physicians. She had spent all that she had, but they could not heal her. She continued to grow steadily worse. In her weakened condition, with great effort, she worked her way through the crowd. If she could just get close enough to reach through the people and touch his clothes, she knew she would be healed. With great faith she extended her arm and touched his robe.

It was a miracle. She felt the strength of her body being restored. She knew she had been healed. Grateful, and not wanting more, she withdrew into the crowd again. But Jesus was aware. He turned and asked, "Who touched my clothes?" Peter wondered how with so many people pressing around he could ask who touched him. But the Savior felt more than the crowd pressing against him. Jesus knew that virtue or strength had gone out of him.

When everyone denied having touched him, the woman with such great faith came forward, trembling. Falling down before the Lord, she confessed what she had done. She explained why she had touched him. She then told all who could hear that she had been healed. She must have been anxious and fearful for all the concern she had caused.

Jesus looked at her and spoke kindly and gently, "Daughter, be of good comfort: thy faith hath made thee whole; go in peace." He wanted her to know that it was not in touching the clothing but rather through her great faith in him that she had been healed. (See *Commentary,* 1:318—19; Luke 8:43—48.)

While on his way to help someone in need, the Savior had stopped to heal another. Jairus, the father of the dying child, must have become very anxious and concerned, but he had placed his trust in the Master and had been willing to wait. They continued on now, but before they reached Jairus's house, messengers met them with the sorrowful news that the child was dead. She had died after her father had gone for help. They reported that it was too late to do anything. Jesus heard their comments, and knowing the anguish of the father, he strengthened Jairus's faith with encouraging words, "Be not afraid, only believe" (Mark 5:36).

As they approached Jairus's house, people were making a loud noise, weeping and crying aloud with the professional mourners as was the custom. Jesus asked the people why they wept with such ado when the daughter wasn't dead but was only sleeping. The mourners were scornful. They laughed at him. If what he said was true, they would lose their opportunity to be paid for mourning.

Jesus then ordered the people to leave so there was an atmosphere of peace and quiet in the house. He allowed no one to enter with him where the child lay except the Apostles, Peter, James, and John, and the sorrowful but trusting father and mother. Approaching the bed and taking the hand of this little twelve-year-old girl in his own, Jesus spoke to her: "Damsel, I say unto thee, arise" (Mark 5:41).

The ruler's daughter opened her eyes. She got up and walked from her bed. Her parents were astonished yet filled with joy. This little girl was their only child and Jesus had restored her to them. Because of him they would be able to love and raise and care for her. Rejoicing and gratitude filled their hearts for Jesus' kindness and for his great power. Jesus, sensitive to every need of the child, kindly instructed the parents to give their young daughter some food. He also told them not to tell anyone what they had experienced.

The mourners probably spread the news throughout the area that the little girl had been restored to life. The crowds following Jesus would now become even greater. The Savior continued to teach and to heal the sick and to make the blind to see and the lame to walk. He expected in return that his followers would do as he asked—"Keep my commandments" (John 14:15). He did not heal people so they could continue their wrongdoing; he wanted them to follow his teachings and become true disciples.

Jesus felt great compassion for the multitudes who followed him, because they did not have the gospel. They were like sheep who had no shepherd to lead them, and there were so many. At this time, he instructed his twelve Apostles and sent them forth, two by two, to declare the gospel message in the cities and villages. They had been taught by the Master. Day after day they had witnessed his use of the healing power of the priesthood and his knowledge and authority as he taught—the greatest missionary of all time. Now Jesus placed in them the highest of all trust and honor as he sent them forth and said, "He that receiveth you receiveth me" (Matthew 10:40).

The twelve special witnesses of Christ set out on their missions, traveling in pairs, while Jesus continued his personal ministry. These humble men, called to be his representatives and to carry his message, went forth with the same power Jesus used. They taught the gospel fearlessly, in plainness. Through the power of the priesthood they also healed the sick and cast out devils. They proclaimed the name of Jesus and his gospel throughout the area.

About this time, Herod Antipas, the wicked ruler of Galilee who had imprisoned John, became so ensnared by lust and pride that he had John beheaded. John the Baptist sealed his testimony with his own blood in defense of Jesus Christ. During his ministry, the forerunner had devotedly shifted his position to that of follower. He had faithfully prepared the way and had with great integrity directed all of his followers to the Lamb of God. Jesus had a great love for John. He had completed his mission of preparation without faltering. Now the Savior must continue with his own ministry, but he expressed to those around him his ultimate tribute to his forerunner: "I say unto you, Among them that are born of women there hath not risen a greater [prophet] than John the Baptist" (Matthew 11:11).

When Herod Antipas heard of the great works performed by Jesus around Galilee, he began to think that Jesus was John brought back to life. He was curious to see Jesus, but the Savior, aware of the danger, left the area for the eastern part of Galilee, where Herod Philip ruled. (See *The Mortal Messiah,* 2:344.)

The Twelve had returned by now and were anxious to report their labors and to bear testimony that through the power of the priesthood which had been conferred upon them, they had been able to do just as they had seen Jesus do—heal the sick, cast out devils, and in every way accomplish the mission to which they had been appointed. But there seemed to be little opportunity for them to be with the Savior privately. There were so many people eager to be near the Master that there wasn't even time for them to eat. The Apostles were then extended a welcome invitation by Jesus, "Come ye yourselves apart into a desert place, and rest a while" (Mark 6:31). Jesus and the Twelve left the throngs of people, entered a boat, and crossed the lake to find temporary seclusion.

    Near the city of Bethsaida-Julias, Jesus and the Apos-
tles found a quiet place on a hillside where they could be
together and converse. (See *Jesus the Christ*, p. 346.) They
had been there only a short while when the group saw the
multitude again coming like sheep without a shepherd.
The crowd had walked all the way around the lake, not
wanting to be apart from the Master. With great compassion and tenderness the Savior responded to their faith
and desires and went to them and continued to teach
them, healing their sick and comforting them. The people
stayed and stayed, not wanting to leave, and were apparently unaware of the passing of time. They had been without food for many hours, and realizing their need, Jesus
was concerned for their physical comfort. When the question arose as to how to provide food for them, Andrew
told Jesus there was a lad present who had five barley
loaves and two small fishes, but he added, "What are they
among so many?" (John 6:9). Some of the Apostles
thought that the people should leave and find food and
lodging in a nearby town, but the Master said they need
not go.

    It was springtime, and the hills in the area were
covered with grass and wild flowers. Jesus instructed the
people to sit together on the grass in groups of fifties and
hundreds. All that he did proceeded in a peaceful, orderly
way. The people followed his instructions and sat down
on the grassy slopes. There were five thousand men
besides women and children who needed to be fed. The
Apostles, even with all their experience with the Master,
must have wondered what Jesus would do with only five
loaves and two fishes.

    Jesus, taking the loaves and fishes, gave a blessing of
thanks on the food. Then he began to distribute it among

the Apostles, who in turn served all the men, women, and children seated on the grassy hillside. Under the Master's touch the fish and bread increased, and the multitude feasted until everyone had enough and to spare. He then asked the disciples to gather up what was left over so nothing would be wasted. There were twelve baskets of surplus.

The people marvelled at the event they had witnessed. Surely this must be the promised Messiah who would care for them and make them again a powerful nation. In their misguided enthusiasm, they wanted to forcibly make Jesus their king. But they understood only their immediate temporal needs. The Savior instructed his disciples to leave by boat, while he remained to dismiss the misdirected multitude. They responded to his request. (See John 6:1–15.)

As dusk came, Jesus climbed a mountain and found a quiet secluded place where he could be alone. Here he prayed to his Father in Heaven, seeking direction and comfort and strength.

During that night a great storm raged. The strong winds made the boat the Apostles were in almost unmanageable. They battled the treacherous waves through the night but made little progress. Jesus, even in his time alone, was aware of them, and he left his brief time of seclusion and came to their rescue by walking out toward them on the stormy sea. When the frightened Apostles saw a man walking on the water, they were filled with fear, thinking it was an apparition. Jesus spoke through the wind and the storm as he comforted his closest associates who had not yet learned all they were to know. They heard his voice through the storm saying, "Be of good cheer; it is I; be not afraid."

Peter was so relieved by hearing the words of the Master that he called back in a strong voice, "Lord, if it be thou, bid me come unto thee on the water." Jesus consented, and Peter got out of the ship onto the water and began walking toward the Master. When the force of the wind hit him and Peter gave his attention to the waves rising around him, his faith weakened, and he began to sink. Even though he was a strong swimmer, he was afraid and called out again through the storm, "Lord, save me." Jesus came to his rescue. When they were in the boat, he helped him understand why he sank, "O thou of little faith, wherefore didst thou doubt?" Peter could have continued safely through the stormy sea if he had kept his faith centered on his Savior. (See Matthew 14:24–31.)

The Apostles were still young in their faith, and although they had just witnessed the miracle of feeding the five thousand, they marvelled at the power of one who could walk on the windswept sea. The frightful voyage ended when the boat arrived somewhere near a beautiful, fertile plain to the south of Capernaum, known as Gennesaret.

Here they went ashore, and the word of the Savior's presence spread quickly. Messengers went to all the people in the area, and they flocked to Jesus, bringing with them those who suffered afflictions. As he visited in the various towns, the sick were laid in the streets in the hope that his passing might heal them. Many "besought him that they might touch if it were but the border of his garment: and as many as touched him were made whole" (Mark 6:56). It was a day of faith and rejoicing.

By now the multitude who the day before had been fed the loaves and fishes were in search of Jesus again. They had taken passage on boats heading to Capernaum, and there they found him. When they spoke to him, wondering how he had crossed the sea in the storm, Jesus gave no accounting but reproved them saying, "Ye seek me, not because ye saw the miracles, but because ye did eat of the loaves, and were filled."

Their concern was for continued access to loaves and fishes—physical food. These people were unlike the followers of Gennesaret who believed the teachings of the Savior and were healed because of their great faith. They were in search of temporal food, and as a result they would leave spiritually hungry. The Lord rebuked them and taught them the truths he wanted them to know: "Labour not for the meat which perisheth, but for that meat which endureth unto everlasting life, which the Son of man shall give unto you" (John 6:26—27).

Jesus was teaching the Jews whose ancestors, the Israelites, God had given manna in the wilderness as Moses led them out of Egypt. At that time this breadlike food had been miraculously provided daily for the Israelites, and now, because of their traditions the Jews felt their long-awaited Messiah would provide bread for them also on a daily basis and sustain life.

Jesus had taught the woman at the well in Samaria, telling her he would give her "living water" so she would never thirst; and now he spoke of the bread of life, saying, "I am the bread of life: he that cometh to me shall never hunger; and he that believeth on me shall never thirst." Jesus further testified, "Except ye eat the flesh of the Son of man, and drink his blood, ye have no life in you" (John 6:35, 53).

Many of the people resisted this teaching. They did not fail to understand the symbolism of Christ's doctrine because of their ignorance. Rather, many chose not to believe that eating the flesh and drinking the blood meant to believe in Jesus and accept him as the Son of God, the Savior of the world, and to obey his commandments. (See *Jesus the Christ*, p. 342.)

When Jesus finished this great public discourse, many people said his teachings were too hard. Jesus knew that what he taught on this occasion would be understood only by the people who had faith in him and who were enlightened by the Spirit. This was a crucial time of testing and sifting between those who would follow the "strong doctrine" and those who would not. It was the beginning of a separation that would continue for ages among all people. It was the separation of those who would follow the Master and walk with him no matter how hard the course and those who chose to fall away.

From that time on, many of his followers turned their backs on Jesus and left him. Even the twelve Apostles did not yet understand the full meaning of this last discourse. His heart must have been heavy as he turned to the Twelve, his chosen friends, and asked, "Will ye also go away?" It was Peter who responded for all of them: "Lord, to whom shall we go? thou hast the words of eternal life" (John 6:67–68).

Chapter 7

"WHOM SAY YE THAT I AM?"

Knowing that the days of his earthly ministry were growing shorter, the Savior desired to prepare and strengthen his Apostles for the trying events ahead. Now walking with him, the Twelve followed the Savior inland from the Sea of Galilee toward Caesarea Philippi. Here were beautiful, cooling springs that fed the Jordan River and the rising foothills of Mount Hermon. Here in solitude the Savior drew his Apostles to him and asked this question: "Whom do men say that I am?" (Mark 8:27).

They answered with what they had heard from the crowds that had left them. Some, they said, were like the superstitious Herod and believed that Jesus was John the Baptist returned to life; others thought he was Elijah or Jeremiah or some other prophet of the Old Testament.

Patiently, the Savior heard their answers, and now weighing their experiences of the past months and desiring to search their souls, he solemnly asked: "But whom say ye that I am?" (Mark 8:28—29).

Peter answered with all the energy of his being, "Thou art the Christ, the Son of the living God" (Matthew 16:16).

Peter's faith must have filled the Savior with great joy. He commended Peter and said, "Blessed art thou, Simon Bar-jona: for flesh and blood hath not revealed it unto thee, but my Father which is in heaven" (Matthew 16:17).

As his Master had hoped, Peter had gained a testimony. Peter had received a knowledge of the truth from a divine source. Though he had pondered and reasoned, heard sermons and seen miracles, all of that could fade and be lost; but this revelation of truth from God through the Holy Ghost was now indelible on his soul.

Jesus explained further to Peter that His Church would be built upon the principle of revelation from God. Just as Peter's testimony would make him strong and immovable as a rock, the principle of revelation would also make the Church and its members strong, even against the power of Satan. (See Matthew 16:18; D&C 33:11—13.)

After this powerful expression of testimony, which Peter bore for himself and in behalf of the other Apostles, the Savior cautioned them against openly declaring him as the Messiah because of the intense hostility of the Jews. His mission among them must continue until he himself would conclude it. The Savior then began to teach the Apostles about his coming death and resurrection.

Having a testimony that Jesus was the Christ did not give the Apostles an automatic understanding of the gospel plan. Peter could only grasp that Jesus had said he was going to die. Because his love for the Savior was very great, Peter told Jesus that he should not let this happen. The Lord rebuked Peter for trying to dissuade him from his mission, and then taught them saying: "Whosoever will come after me, let him deny himself, and take up his cross, and follow me. . . . Whosoever shall be willing to lose his life for my sake, and the gospel, the same shall save it. For what shall it profit a man if he shall gain the whole world, and lose his own soul? . . . Therefore deny yourselves of these, and be not ashamed of me" (JST Mark 8:36, 38—40).

The Apostles were learning that choosing to follow the Savior and walk with him meant giving up some of the things that they wanted desperately to cling to. Ideas, habits, relationships, and even one's life might be required; but the Savior was also giving up all that he had. He would suffer for the sins of all mankind and give his own life in order to offer his followers eternal life and a place in his kingdom.

During those next few days, Jesus continued to teach and strengthen his Apostles, and they asked him many questions. Toward the end of a week's time, on an early evening, he took with him Peter, James, and John and "went up into a mountain to pray."

The climb brought them to cooler, fresher air. Beautiful vistas opened and closed to their view as they moved upward. Reaching a place which he felt was appropriate and secluded, the Savior began to pray. Peter, James, and John, weary from the exertion, "were heavy with sleep." But soon, something startled them into wakefulness. There in the darkness of the night, they beheld their Master transfigured before them. His clothing was as white as light, and his face shone like the sun. There were two other glorified beings with the Lord

—Moses and Elijah, prophet leaders of the Old Testament. They spoke with him about his coming atonement and the final events of his life which would occur in Jerusalem. (See Luke 9:28—32.)

The sacred events taking place on the mountain reached a glorious climax when a cloud of light overshadowed the three Apostles, and they heard the voice of God the Eternal Father saying: "This is my beloved Son, in whom I am well pleased; hear ye him."

At the sound of the voice of the Father, the Apostles fell to the ground and hid their faces. When the experience had passed, it was Jesus who gently touched them and said, "Arise, and be not afraid." (See Matthew 17:5—7.)

Peter, James, and John did arise—to a greater trust and an increased responsibility. On this holy mountain they received the keys of the kingdom of heaven, the power and authority to preside over and direct the affairs of Christ's Church. (See *Commentary* 1:399—404.) They would become the First Presidency for their day. Moses bestowed the keys of the gathering of Israel and Elijah the keys of the sealing power so that baptisms and other ordinances of the priesthood done here on earth would also be valid after this life. Moses and Elijah also represented the law and the prophets which had been given to prepare Israel for the coming of Christ. (See Galatians 3:24.) Old dispensations were now past; the gospel dispensation was now established by Jesus Christ, and the Father himself had commanded, "Hear ye him."

The sacred experience on the mountain was concluded. The fervent prayer of the Savior had been answered. With the coming of the new day, they descended from the mountain, and the Savior instructed the three

Apostles not to tell others of their experience until after he had risen from the dead.

Though they had participated in the marvelous events of the night before, they and the rest of the Twelve needed further preparation for the time when they must shoulder the responsibility of the Lord's kingdom themselves, and he continued to teach them. When some of the Apostles who had not been with him on the mountain tried to heal a boy of an evil spirit and were unsuccessful, the Savior instructed them to strengthen their faith through fasting. (See Matthew 17:14—21.) Greater power was needed to overcome this evil spirit, just as greater power is needed to overcome some weaknesses and sins. The Apostles learned that fasting is a way to focus and increase faith and to draw on divine help to overcome evil and to receive inspiration.

As they traveled toward Capernaum, the Savior again taught them of his coming death and resurrection. Still they resisted these teachings and could not understand them because of their fear. But as Jews, they did understand the general expectation that the Messiah would establish his kingdom, and along the way they began to first speculate and then to argue concerning what positions they would have in it.

On their arrival at the house, the Savior, though he already knew their thoughts, asked the Apostles, "What was it that ye disputed among yourselves by the way?" (Mark 9:33).

A sudden silence came over them. None wished to answer him.

The Savior sat down and lovingly called the Apostles around him and said, "If any man desire to be first, the same shall be last of all, and servant of all" (Mark 9:35).

Then he called a child in the room to him. Jesus gently took the child into his arms and taught his Apostles: "Except ye be converted, and become as little children, ye shall not enter into the kingdom of heaven. Whosoever therefore shall humble himself as this little child, the same is greatest in the kingdom of heaven" (Matthew 18:3—4).

His followers must learn to be like children — trusting, obedient, pure, full of faith, humble, and teachable. If they could develop such godly attributes in themselves, their service would be acceptable. No matter what position they held, they would be true servants of the Master.

Questions and answers continued to be exchanged as the apostles learned. Peter asked, "Lord, how oft shall my brother sin against me, and I forgive him? till seven times?"

The Savior replied and told a story. A king called his servants to him to make an accounting. One of the servants owed the king ten thousand talents. There was no way he could possibly pay so large a debt. The king commanded that the servant and his wife and children be sold into slavery and all his possessions likewise be sold to make the payment. The servant fell down and worshipped the king. He pleaded for patience and mercy, promising to pay back all that was owed. The king was deeply touched by this appeal. He forgave the servant of his debt and released him to freedom.

Now this same servant went out and found a fellow servant who owed him only a hundred pence. He threatened him, took him by the throat, and demanded his money. His fellow servant fell down in front of him and pleaded for patience and mercy, promising to pay all that was owed. But he would not listen, and put him in prison until the debt would be paid. When the king was told about this event, he called the wicked servant to him again. He reminded him that when he had pleaded for mercy, he had been forgiven of his great debt. Shouldn't he have been as merciful to his debtor? The king then delivered the wicked servant to the tormentors until he should pay all that was due him. Then the Savior concluded: "So likewise shall my heavenly Father do also unto you, if ye from your hearts forgive not every one his brother their trespasses." (See Matthew 18:21–35.)

Should Peter forgive just seven times? He was taught by his Lord that the merciful would obtain mercy, and harsh punishment would follow those who dealt harshly with others. With each question and answer, each story and illustration, the Master lifted his followers to a greater insight and a higher plane of behavior and prepared them for the greater responsibility that would follow.

Each of the Twelve received the keys of the kingdom (Matthew 18:18), and as the work grew, the Savior called more laborers. These were the seventies. He sent them "two and two before his face into every city and place, whither he himself would come" (Luke 10:1). The seventies' calling was to assist the Twelve Apostles in the work of the Church. They too bore testimony of Jesus Christ and helped to carry the gospel to those who hungered for its message.

Now the great Galilean ministry was drawing to its close. Jesus would not pass again through the country of his youth, the fertile valleys, the grassy hills and meadows, the mountain tops, the glistening Sea of Galilee. He must do the will of his Father. His course was set toward Jerusalem.

Chapter 8

"I AM THE LIGHT OF THE WORLD"

A touch of gold had appeared on the leaves. The early autumn air was cool and pleasant. With the harvest of the fields and vines now gathered, the Jews turned their energies to the celebration of the Feast of Tabernacles. During these beautiful autumn days there would be many guests and visitors coming to Jerusalem. They must build booths or shelters (tabernacles) from branches of living trees. These leafy tents in their courtyards or on the rooftops would be their dwelling places during the week of the feast. Here they would sleep, eat, study, and pray. The temporary living in the tabernacles was to remind them of the days when Israel journeyed in the wilderness with Moses and had no permanent home; and the gathered harvest marked not only a time of thanksgiving, but looked forward to a final gathering, when the harvest would be of nations and people returned to the Lord.

The streets of Jerusalem were becoming crowded with visitors, especially those who came from great distances and even neighboring lands. All day long the smoke from the additional sacrifices hovered in the air over the great temple. A greater number of priests than usual were involved in the ceremonies, and throngs of people participated or looked on.

"Where is he?" was the low murmur on the lips of the people. They were curious and agitated as they wondered if Jesus would come to Jerusalem to the feast. They discussed their opinions of him with each other. Some thought he was a good man; others thought he was deceiving the people. But they kept their opinions quietly among themselves for fear of their rulers.

Then, midway during the days of the feast, Jesus arrived and "went up into the temple, and taught." The people listened intently. The Jewish teachers were amazed, so much so that they questioned among themselves, "How knoweth this man letters, having never learned?" Jesus was not a graduate of their schools of the rabbis. They had received their training by tradition passed from one great rabbinical teacher to another and claiming to reach back to Moses. But where had this tradesman, this uneducated Galilean, learned?

Jesus answered their troubled questions saying, "My doctrine is not mine, but his that sent me." Then, knowing they would dispute it, he offered this test: "If any man will do his will, he shall know of the doctrine, whether it be of God, or whether I speak of myself." The burden of proof was placed on the listeners. It was an invitation as well. Try the doctrine, introduce it into your very being. Live it, and you will know. (See John 7:14–17; David O. McKay, in Conference Report, Oct.

1966, p. 136.) The Savior continued his teaching, and no one dared oppose him. "Did not Moses give you the law, and yet none of you keepeth the law?" (John 7:19.) "Judge not according to your traditions, but judge righteous judgment" (JST John 7:24).

Now the people began to wonder. Wasn't this the man the rulers sought to kill? Why did they let him speak so boldly and do nothing?

When the chief priests and Pharisees heard the people begin to speak of Jesus as possibly the Christ, they feared a demonstration in favor of Jesus. Quickly they dispatched the temple guards to watch for the right moment and seize him.

Jesus was not intimidated but taught even more pointedly. On each of the first seven days of the feast, if not the eighth and last, a procession of priests brought water in a golden vessel from the Pool of Siloam to the altar in the temple. As they came toward the altar, the trumpets sounded. This was the high point of the temple ceremony. As the water was poured out, the words of Jehovah to ancient Israel were sung: "With joy shall ye draw water out of the wells of salvation" (Isaiah 12:3). At some time during the celebration, no doubt having this ceremony in mind, Jesus cried aloud, "If any man thirst, let him come unto me, and drink" (John 7:37).

Jesus was making an open claim to the Messiahship. Only he could offer salvation to mankind, and he identified himself as its source. When the people heard this teaching, many began to say he was the Christ.

The guards also heard all his sayings and returned to the chief priests and Pharisees subdued and without a prisoner. Angrily, those leaders questioned, "Why have ye not brought him?"

They answered truthfully: "Never man spake like this man."

Furious at the reply, the leaders accused the guards of being deceived. They demeaned the common people and called them cursed for their lack of learning and their belief in Christ.

A voice among them was then raised in measured protest. It was Nicodemus, the member of the Sanhedrin who had come to Jesus at night to learn of his teachings. He questioned the legality of their actions, "Doth our law judge any man, before it hear him, and know what he doeth?" Enraged, they turned on him and countered, "Art thou also of Galilee?" (See John 7:45–52.)

The incident ended. Each man withdrew to his own home. The opportunity that presented itself to Nicodemus to strongly testify for Jesus was past. The moment had faded in the press of daily life.

The Savior continued to teach in the temple. As a part of the celebration now concluding, four great lamp-stands had been set out in the temple courts. Their candles had burned brightly during the temple illumination. Jesus again drew on his immediate surroundings and taught, saying, "I am the light of the world: he that followeth me shall not walk in darkness, but shall have the light of life" (John 8:12). Here in the temple over thirty years earlier, Jesus as a baby had been taken into the arms of Simeon and recognized and blessed as the "light to lighten the Gentiles, and the glory of thy people Israel" (Luke 2:32). Now he stood before them, fulfilling prophecy. He was that light, their Messiah.

The Savior's concluding teachings at the temple were filled with unveiled truth. He taught of his relationship to his Father and foretold of his crucifixion: "When ye have lifted up the Son of man, then shall ye know that I am he, and that I do nothing of myself; but as my Father hath taught me, I speak these things. And he that sent me is with me: the Father hath not left me alone; for I do always those things that please him."

To the Jews who believed in him he said: "If ye continue in my word, then are ye my disciples indeed; And ye shall know the truth, and the truth shall make you free." Freedom from sin is obtained only through knowing and obeying the gospel of Christ. Many of the Jews did not understand and felt that Jesus had referred to them as slaves. They became offended, for they claimed Abraham as their father and said they had never been in bondage to any man. How conveniently they had forgotten the four centuries of bondage in Egypt and their long captivity in Babylon. And even now there were Roman soldiers looking down over the temple from their fortress above them.

Jesus said to them: "If ye were Abraham's children, ye would do the works of Abraham. But now ye seek to kill me, a man that hath told you the truth."

His truth angered them, and voices from the crowd called him possessed of a devil. Wanting to completely separate themselves from him, they hurled their ultimate insult and called him a Samaritan.

Jesus continued: "Your father Abraham rejoiced to see my day: and he saw it, and was glad." (See John 8:28–56.)

How little they knew of Abraham. He had indeed looked forward in time almost two thousand years and saw in vision the coming of Jesus Christ and rejoiced in that future day when the Savior would atone for the sins of the world. (See JST Genesis 15:12.)

Again misunderstanding, the people jeered and said,

"Thou art not yet fifty years old, and hast thou seen Abraham?"

Jesus answered saying: "Verily, verily, I say unto you, Before Abraham was, I am" (John 8:57—58).

There could be no misunderstanding this answer. Jesus openly confronted them with the fact that he was Jehovah, who was identified to Moses by the name I AM. (See Exodus 3:13—14; 6:2—3.) Jewish tradition forbade that the sacred name even be spoken. Jesus had not only used it, but he claimed it as his own.

The Jews were so enraged by his answer that they took up rocks from the construction work in the temple courts and would have immediately stoned him, but he hid himself and left the temple. Never had the people been taught so openly of his divine identity, and how the powers of darkness rebelled against that light!

Out in the crowded streets of the city of Jerusalem, probably near an entrance to the temple, there sat alone a man who was a beggar. Daily he reached out and spoke to the passing people, asking for alms. Though he could hear them, he saw nothing, for his was a world of darkness. He had been born blind.

Jesus and the disciples passed that way on the Sabbath and saw the sightless man in his accustomed place. The disciples were struck with a question and asked, "Master, who did sin, this man, or his parents, that he was born blind?"

Jesus answered, "Neither hath this man sinned, nor his parents: but that the works of God should be made manifest in him" (John 9:2—3).

The Savior then spat on the ground and made clay. The beggar could only feel the gentle touch of the Savior's hands as he anointed his eyes, but with that touch, he then readily accepted the command of his voice: "Go, wash in the pool of Siloam."

The beggar went. He washed, and he returned seeing. The Savior was gone, but neighbors and others who knew the beggar from seeing him so many years in his accustomed place ran to him. As the excitement spread, people gathered around him. Some would not believe it was the same beggar, but he reassured them.

They asked him, "How were thine eyes opened?" And he answered, "A man that is called Jesus made clay, and anointed mine eyes, and said unto me, Go to the pool of Siloam, and wash: and I went and washed, and I received sight."

Now, because this healing had been done on the Sabbath day, the beggar was brought before the Pharisees for questioning. They wanted to discredit the miracle and accuse Jesus. When they asked the beggar how he had received his sight, he said simply, "He put clay upon mine eyes, and I washed, and do see."

The Pharisees told the beggar that Jesus could not be a man of God, because he broke the Sabbath by healing him on that day. Others of them said, "How can a man that is a sinner do such miracles?"

Then they asked the beggar his opinion of Jesus. He answered, "He is a prophet."

The beggar's answers were not bringing the hoped-for result, so the Pharisees tried next to prove that the man had not really been blind. They called his parents for questioning.

The parents were fearful. The rulers had declared that if any man said Jesus was the Christ, he would be excommunicated from the synagogue. That meant that no one in the community would have anything to do with them; at the worst, they would be considered as if they were dead.

The parents assured the Pharisees that the beggar was their son and that he had been born blind. But when they asked how he was now able to see, the parents carefully denied any knowledge of who healed him and said, "He is of age; ask him."

Now the Pharisees called the beggar again and sweepingly suggested: "Give God the praise: we know that this man is a sinner." But the man fearlessly replied, "Whether he be a sinner or no, I know not: one thing I know, that, whereas I was blind, now I see."

They tried again to have the man admit how he had been healed and hoped that he would contradict himself in retelling his story. "What did he to thee? how opened he thine eyes?" they demanded.

He answered with emphasis: "I have told you already: . . . wherefore would ye hear it again? will ye also be his disciples?"

They were outraged at this answer. "We are Moses' disciples. We know that God spake unto Moses: as for this fellow, we know not from whence he is."

The beggar went on: "Why herein is a marvellous thing," said he, "that ye know not from whence he is, and yet he hath opened mine eyes. Now we know that God heareth not sinners: but if any man be a worshipper of God, and doeth his will, him he heareth. Since the world began was it not heard that any man opened the eyes of one that was born blind. If this man were not of God, he could do nothing."

Maddened but weakened, these learned men haughtily responded to the beggar, "Thou wast altogether born in sins, and dost thou teach us?"

Defeated in the skills of argumentation and question-ing for which they were renouned, the Pharisees now re-treated to their official authority and unjustly pronounced the beggar excommunicated.

By all customs and standards the beggar was now isolated from the congregation and the community. He was reviled and avoided. But one came, seeking him out, who would not forsake him, "Dost thou believe on the Son of God?"

The beggar answered, "Who is he, Lord, that I might believe on him?"

And Jesus said to him, "Thou hast both seen him, and it is he that talketh with thee."

Now the outcast beggar recognized the voice, and in the brightness of the noonday, seeing him said, "Lord, I believe." And he worshipped him. (See John 9:6—38.)

Chapter 9

TOWARD JERUSALEM
AND THE CROSS

The events of the Feast of Tabernacles showed the inability of the Jewish religious leaders to spiritually nourish or care for the people who hungered and thirsted for the things of God. Because of their hard hearts and lack of understanding, they were more likely to cast those people out, as they did the healed blind man, than they were to gather them or care for their greatest needs. (See Ezekiel 34:1–10.)

All of these things caused a deep sadness in the Savior as he continued to teach his people. At this time he spoke to them about a part of life in Palestine that was familiar to all of them and that all could understand—the work of the shepherds.

Each evening the shepherds gathered the sheep together into a sheepfold. The high walls of this enclosure would keep them safe during the night. Branches of thorn bushes were placed at the top of the walls to keep wolves from jumping into the enclosure. A single door allowed the sheep to go in or come out, and one shepherd took a turn each night to guard the door while the others went home to rest.

Often, more than one flock of sheep would be brought into the fold. In the morning, when the other shepherds returned, the doorkeeper would recognize them. Each shepherd was then allowed to enter and call his sheep. Each sheep recognized its own shepherd's voice. As the sheep were called, the shepherd led them out into the fields to pasture.

Now the Savior taught them, saying, "I am the door: by me if any man enter in, he shall be saved, and shall go in and out, and find pasture" (John 10:9). Through the atonement, the Savior would provide the way for us to enter his kingdom, to find safety and peace both on earth and in heaven. He is the door, and there is no other through which we can enter.

Jesus explained that others might try to climb up into the fold some other way. They were like thieves and robbers who try to steal and kill and destroy the sheep. But "I am come that they might have life, and that they might have it more abundantly" (John 10:10). The truths the Savior taught were not only to help us gain salvation in an eternal kingdom, but to give us happiness here on earth. When the principles of the gospel were taught for the first time on this earth to Adam, he understood this and exclaimed, "In *this* life I shall have joy, and again in the flesh I shall see God" (Moses 5:10; italics added). As the Savior observed the work of the Pharisees and the other false shepherds of his people and saw how his sheep hungered for nourishment under their empty teachings and their endless applications of the Mosaic law, he longed for them all to understand and accept his gospel and to have life more abundantly.

"I am the good shepherd," he continued, "and know my sheep, and am known of mine, . . . And I lay down my life for the sheep. . . . No man taketh it from me, but I lay it down of myself. I have power to lay it down, and I have power to take it again. This commandment have I received of my Father" (John 10:14—15, 18).

The love of the Shepherd is so personal that he knows each of us by name. It is so strong that he is willing to give his own life for us. No one could take the Savior's life from him. From his mother, Mary, a mortal woman, he had received the capacity to die. From God, his immortal Father, he had received the capacity to live and conquer death. His atonement would be a voluntary sacrifice made possible by this dual inheritance.

Referring again to the work of the shepherds, the Savior taught, "And other sheep I have, which are not of this fold: them also I must bring, and they shall hear my voice; and there shall be one fold, and one shepherd" (John 10:16).

The "other sheep" that the Savior referred to were also a part of the house of Israel. Some of them, descendants of Joseph of Egypt, had been led away from Jerusalem six hundred years before the birth of Christ. The Lord directed this group of Israelites, through their prophet-leader Lehi, to leave Jerusalem to escape captivity and bondage. The mission of Jesus Christ would include such scattered sheep of Israel, and they would also be privileged to hear the voice of their Shepherd and to be gathered again into the fold. (See 3 Nephi 16:1—3.)

The coat worn by shepherds of that day often had a large pocket sewn inside it. A wounded or weak lamb could be put in it and carried to safety. The love and mission of the Savior were of such magnitude that he would call the weak and the strong, every nation and people to him. As the prophet Isaiah foresaw, "He shall feed his flock like a shepherd: he shall gather the lambs with his arm, and carry them in his bosom" (Isaiah 40:11).

The Savior concluded his teachings at the Feast of Tabernacles and the Feast of Dedication with a sorrowful heart. Again he had been rejected by the majority of the people, and again his life had been threatened. Now, in the last months of his mortal ministry, he crossed the Jordan into the area known as Perea. Here the Savior's teachings were intensified, and he chose to draw sharp contrasts between the religious practices of the Jews and the life-giving principles of his gospel.

Often he mingled with sinners and with publicans—those Jews who accepted office with the Roman government and helped collect the hated taxes. The Pharisees and scribes criticized Jesus for his attention to this class of people that they carefully avoided and despised. But through the parables of the lost sheep, the lost coin, and the prodigal son, Jesus taught that every soul was of great value in the kingdom of God. Those who have the trust and responsibility to lead others must display the love of the Shepherd and recover the lost sheep as well as keep safe the ninety and nine. Like the widow who found the lost coin, each member of the Church must cherish and value the worth of the other and see that none is lost inadvertently. And the Savior taught that should one choose to wilfully leave his Father and waste his inheritance in sin, his repentant return should be greeted with rejoicing and acceptance. Thus he illustrated the worth of souls to the Father and the love his disciples should have for each other. (See Luke 15:3—32.)

Jesus received a message while he was teaching in Perea. It came from Bethany, a town about two miles from Jerusalem. Jesus had spent many happy hours in Bethany at the home of Mary and Martha, who were sisters, and Lazarus, their brother. There he found temporary rest from his labors and enjoyed a close spiritual companionship with these beloved friends. But something had happened in their family. Lazarus was very ill, and Jesus now received a message sent by Mary and Martha with this humble appeal: "Lord, behold, he whom thou lovest is sick." Jesus knew that during the time the messenger was on his way to him, Lazarus had died, but that this event had occurred "for the glory of God."

The Savior chose to remain in Perea for two more days after receiving the message from Mary and Martha. Then he said to his disciples, "Let us go into Judaea again." Surprised and astonished, they replied, "Master, the Jews . . . sought to stone thee; and goest thou thither again?" The scenes of the maddened, angry Jews grasping for stones in the temple to hurl at their master were still vivid in their minds. Yet Jesus was as calm now as he was then, and he gently explained that he must work all the hours of the days designated to him for his ministry. Lazarus was dead, and he must now go to him.

Though a return to Judea made him and the other disciples anxious, when he saw that his Master was determined to go, Thomas voiced his loyalty to his fellow disciples: "Let us also go, that we may die with him." (See John 11:3—16.)

After a day's journey, Jesus arrived in Bethany. Lazarus had already been in the grave for four days. Lazarus and Mary and Martha apparently were members of a family of prominence, and there were many who came to comfort them at the loss of their brother. Martha, when she heard Jesus was coming, went out to meet him, while Mary stayed with the friends and mourners.

Martha's words to the Savior were filled with great faith and testimony: "Lord, if thou hadst been here, my brother had not died. But I know, that even now, whatsoever thou wilt ask of God, God will give it thee."

Jesus replied, "Thy brother shall rise again."

Martha answered from the faith and knowledge she had gained from the Savior's teachings and the testimony of the Holy Ghost: "I know that he shall rise again in the resurrection at the last day."

Then Jesus testified in the majesty of his divine sonship: "I am the resurrection, and the life: he that believeth in me, though he were dead, yet shall he live: And whosoever liveth and believeth in me shall never die. Believest thou this?"

And Martha answered him with all her heart: "Yea, Lord: I believe that thou art the Christ, the son of God, which should come into the world."

After this meeting and exchange of deepest feeling, Martha went back to the house and told Mary secretly that Jesus had arrived. Mary quickly left to go to the Master. The guests, thinking Mary was going to the grave to mourn, followed her.

When Mary caught sight of Jesus, she ran to him and fell at his feet weeping. She too exclaimed, "Lord, if thou hadst been here, my brother had not died."

When Jesus saw her weeping and the Jews who were with her, he groaned within himself and asked simply, "Where have ye laid him?" As they led him to the garden and the cave where the body lay entombed, the Savior wept silently. Some of the observing Jews said, "Behold how he loved him!" But others who wanted to belittle his power questioned why he could heal a man born blind but not prevent the death of his friend. Jesus heard these comments as they approached the grave. Perceiving those filled with hatred mingled with those who truly sorrowed and seeing also the stark effects of death, he was again overcome with emotion and groaned within himself.

Now, as he stood before the sealed tomb, Jesus said, "Take ye away the stone." The request to be shown the place of burial and the request to reopen the grave were tests of faith. Martha became fearful. She knew her brother's body had already been dead for four days and would have begun to decompose and smell, and she told this to Jesus. He then questioned and reminded her, "Said I not unto thee, that, if thou wouldest believe, thou shouldest see the glory of God?" Martha was reassured, and the stone was rolled away.

Reverently the Son of God stood before the opened tomb, and in perfect harmony with his Father addressed him in prayer: "Father, I thank thee that thou hast heard me. And I knew that thou hearest me always: but because of the people which stand by I said it, that they may believe that thou hast sent me."

Then he called with a loud voice, "Lazarus, come forth." Lazarus, in the spirit world heard the voice of the Son of God who had power over life and death, and he obeyed and came forth. His body was still wrapped in white with the napkin about his head, but he was vibrant and living, and the Savior gave instructions to loose him from the graveclothes. (See John 11:3—44.)

The miracle of restoring Lazarus to life could not be refuted. There were witnesses to his death, the preparation of the body, and the burial. And all saw how Jesus called the spirit back to the body after its four-day absence. Part of the witnessing Jews were filled with belief. But even as they and the family members rejoiced together, others who had watched and whose hearts were evil left immediately for Jerusalem to report the incident to the Pharisees and rulers.

Hastily a meeting of the Sanhedrin was called. This latest miracle could not be explained away. What Jesus had done was undeniably something the predicted Messiah would be able to do. If he were allowed to continue, these religious leaders feared he would be accepted as the Messiah and they would lose their place of wealth and prominence among the people. The Romans would then destroy their nation for following one who claimed to be their king.

Caiaphas was the high priest that year, appointed to his calling by the Romans through bribery. It was he who commanded the attention of the discordant Sanhedrin now and suggested the way to stop the miracles. They would slay Jesus. And so the entrusted religious leaders of Israel plotted how they could kill the Son of God.

Jesus and the Twelve quietly left Bethany and went to a small village away from Jerusalem called Ephraim. Here he stayed with his disciples in seclusion until it was time to begin his last journey.

In the early spring, when the Passover was near, Jesus was ready to go up to Jerusalem for the last time, probably with some of his followers from Galilee. The journey was filled with manifestations of the Savior's love and power—he taught in parables, healed lepers, and blessed little children. Once more, in moments of deep solemnity, he taught his apostles of his coming crucifixion. Again their minds were veiled, for those events were to be a test for them, and only after would they clearly understand all that had transpired.

At Jericho the people came out into the streets to greet the Savior and his company. Large crowds thronged and followed him. Here the Lord healed blind Bartimeus (see Mark 10:46—52) and visited Zaccheus, a man short in stature who had climbed a tree in order to catch a glimpse of Jesus passing by. He was a publican who was then honored to have Christ as a guest in his home. As he was taught, Zaccheus repented and was converted. He knew he could not change his past deeds of extortion and fraud, but he determined to do all that was possible to restore what he had taken, even "fourfold," and to be a helper of the poor rather than their oppressor. When the Savior left the next morning, Zaccheus's life had been transformed. (See Luke 19:1—10.)

As Jesus' party left the oasis city, they made their way along the Jericho road through the desolate hill country and began the three-thousand-foot ascent to Jerusalem. Jesus passed near the area of his temptation where he had confronted Satan at the beginning of his ministry. Subtly the tempter was at work again. During this journey Jesus' followers seemed to expect that he was going to Jerusalem to begin his reign as the Messiah and King and to establish a political kingdom. (See Luke 19:11.) Some even asked what positions they might hold in it. Again he patiently taught them that service was the key to their salvation, the means through which their priesthood would be magnified. They were to labor with their fellowmen, for even the "Son of man came not to be ministered unto, but to minister." (See Matthew 20:20—28.)

When the Savior arrived in Bethany, just two miles outside of Jerusalem, it was Friday, six days before the Passover feast. He stayed with his beloved friends Mary and Martha and Lazarus. On Saturday a supper was prepared for him under Martha's direction. Knowing he was there, many people came out from Jerusalem to see him and to see the man raised from the dead. The miracle performed on Lazarus was a source of faith and conversion to many. But this living miracle caused such anguish to the Sanhedrin, that they began to scheme to cause Lazarus's death.

While Jesus was with his intimate friends on this evening, Mary quietly slipped away to her own treasures and returned with a pound of ointment of spikenard in an alabaster container. The ointment was considered very precious and had a fragrant odor. Responding to the Spirit and wanting in some way to express her great love for the Savior—perhaps realizing he was about to leave them— she opened the container and poured out the precious spikenard onto his head and feet and wiped them with her hair. This solemn, loving act was performed by a mortal on the Son of God. Thus was their Messiah and King anointed.

No one should have questioned such an act on this occasion. But Judas Iscariot, the apostle who was the treasurer for the Twelve, said indignantly, "Why was not this ointment sold for three hundred pence, and given to the poor?" (John 12:5). His objection was hypocritical. Concern for the poor was not the motivation for Judas's criticism; his heart was filled with greed. He saw an opportunity to add money to the treasury of the group which he controlled—money which he sometimes used to serve his own purposes. These evil thoughts crowded out the impressions of the Spirit and left Judas completely insensitive to the sacredness of Mary's act and the occasion.

The Savior graciously responded in Mary's behalf and placed all in its proper perspective. "Why trouble ye her? For she hath wrought a good work on me. Ye have the poor with you always, and whensoever ye will, ye may do them good; but me ye have not always. . . . This which she has done unto me, shall be had in remembrance in generations to come, wheresoever my gospel shall be preached: for verily she has come beforehand to anoint my body to the burying" (JST Mark 14:6—8).

The following day was Sunday, and Jesus set out for Jerusalem. Along the way he directed two of his disciples to bring him a young donkey. When they returned with the colt, everything having taken place as Jesus had described, they spread their coats on the animal and Jesus mounted. With him riding in their midst, they proceeded toward the city.

As they descended along the Mount of Olives, increasing crowds gathered around the Savior. The word had gone ahead, and another group came out of the city and joined with the first. The people were jubilant and carried palm fronds. They laid out the fronds and their coats, carpeting his path, as was customary in welcoming a king. The disciples "began to rejoice and praise God with a loud voice . . . Saying, Blessed be the King that cometh in the name of the Lord" (Luke 19:37—38), "Hosanna to the Son of David" (Matthew 21:15), "Hosanna: Blessed is the King of Israel." (John 12:13.)

In the acclamation and uproar the Pharisees were powerless to stop Jesus as he entered the city, but they could not tolerate the people praising him and calling him Messiah and King. In desperation, some of them pushed and pressed their way through the crowds to him and demanded, "Master, rebuke thy disciples." Jesus answered, "I tell you that, if these should hold their peace, the stones would immediately cry out" (Luke 19:39—40). Prophecy was being fulfilled this day (see Zechariah 9:9), and if the testimonies of the disciples were silenced, creation itself—the rocks, trees, valleys, and mountains—would cry out and witness their Creator, the Messiah and King!

Chapter 10

THE LAST PUBLIC TEACHING

The city was in an uproar. Jesus, the "prophet of Nazareth" (Matthew 21:11), had come to the Passover feast. The rulers had commanded beforehand that if anyone saw him, they should come and tell the chief priest and Pharisees so they could arrest him. But Jesus had arrived riding in triumph into the city! Everyone saw him —and the rulers dared not arrest him because of the crowds following him and shouting "Hosanna" as they worshipped him.

Among the great throngs of people in the city were those who were converts to Judaism from other nations. Some of them had come from far-off Greece to be at the Passover. After the triumphal entry and during the time that Jesus was teaching in the temple, "certain ones" of the Greeks desired the opportunity to meet and talk with Jesus. They made their request to the Apostle Philip. He and Andrew then approached the Master, who graciously granted the interview.

From the things Jesus taught them, the Greeks learned that the gospel was to reach all men of all nations: "If any man serve me, him will my Father honour." Salvation is offered to all mankind through obedience to the laws and ordinances of the gospel of Christ.

The Savior then drew an illustration from nature to gently teach and testify of his coming death and atonement. "Except a corn of wheat fall into the ground and die, it abideth alone: but if it die, it bringeth forth much fruit." He would sacrifice his life to give eternal life to all who would accept his gospel and obey its principles and ordinances. These his Father would honor.

As the Savior concluded this teaching, the realization of the nearness of his sacrifice and the sins of those about him, which he would take upon himself, caused him to feel great sorrow. He struggled within himself: "Now is my soul troubled; and what shall I say? Father, save me from this hour: but for this cause came I unto this hour." Reaching out to the only one who could grant him the strength to endure, he prayed, "Father, glorify thy name." He had no desire to escape his promises.

To this prayer of complete submission there came an audible answer from the Father: "I have both glorified it, and will glorify it again." The people who were with the Savior had different impressions of this experience. Some heard with their physical senses a sound, which they interpreted as thunder, and were left uninspired. Others heard with their physical senses and a cultivated spiritual sensitivity a voice, and they came away edified. (See John 12:24—28.)

On Monday morning as the Savior and his Twelve reentered the city from Bethany, he went to the temple to teach. Here he was confronted, as he had been three years before at the Passover, with the noise and filth of the animal sacrifices being bought and sold and the money changers haggling and cheating at their trade. Again, sickened and saddened and righteously angry, he drove them out, overturning the tables, loosing the animals, and stopping those who were carrying merchandise through the sacred temple courts as if the courts were the city streets. He cried aloud, "It is written, My house shall be called the house of prayer; but ye have made it a den of thieves" (Matthew 21:13).

This was the Lord Jehovah speaking. It was his house where he had come to teach during the final days and hours of his earthly ministry. And then, as the house was cleared and the courts became more quiet and reverent, those who could rightfully seek a refuge there came. They—the blind and the lame—emerged from behind the pillars and the porches, and they made their weary way to his side to be healed.

Those who were Jesus' followers watched their Savior minister with tenderness to the physical and spiritual needs of his people. Again the Spirit was manifest to them, and they broke into shouts of "Hosanna," praising and witnessing him as their King and promised Messiah. (See Matthew 21:14—15.)

As Jesus left the city that evening to find rest at Bethany, the chief priests and officials found no peace. Their hearts burned with anger and hatred toward this Galilean who called their temple his house. They would not be ignored. Into the night they schemed, plotting how they could stop Jesus from teaching and reclaim their guardianship over the temple.

The following day, Tuesday, as the Savior began to teach and his followers gathered around him in the temple, a delegation of chief priests, scribes, and representatives of the Sanhedrin approached him. For three years they had questioned, demanded signs, and sought to arrest him. Today, they planned to very simply discredit him before the people, questioning his authority. Then they would arrest him.

As the common people drew back to avoid contaminating these "holy" men by brushing against their clothing, the leaders demanded of Jesus, "By what authority doest thou these things? and who gave thee this authority?" (Matthew 21:23).

The Savior, already aware of their motives, answered them: "I will also ask of you one question, and answer me, and I will tell you by what authority I do these things. The baptism of John, was it from heaven, or of men? answer me" (Mark 11:29—30).

The self-assured leaders were suddenly disarmed. Their own weapon had been turned against them. Embarrassed, they quickly conferred together as to how they could answer the Savior to recover their advantage. If they answered that John's ministry and baptisms were performed with heavenly authority, then Jesus would ask them why they had not believed John. If they denied John's authority, they feared the anger of the people, for the masses accepted John as a prophet. So these learned rulers, whose word had come to be accepted as final in all religious matters, had to weakly answer, "We cannot tell."

Jesus replied, "Neither do I tell you by what authority I do these things" (Mark 11:33).

Now Jesus, whom they sought to question and humiliate, became their teacher. They were unwilling pupils, for each of the three parables he then taught exposed them before the people as hypocritical, unrepentant and unworthy in their callings. (See Matthew 21:28—46; 22:1—14.)

Three groups in turn then carefully confronted the Savior. The Herodians, who supported the Roman government, and the Pharisees tried to engage him in a political question. But the Savior masterfully answered them, "Render therefore unto Caesar the things which are Caesar's; and unto God the things that are God's." (See Matthew 22:15—22.)

The Saduccees, who did not believe in the resurrection, posed a religious question hoping to show that the doctrine of a resurrection was absurd. The Savior answered them, "Ye do err, not knowing the scriptures, nor the power of God." Then he who is the Resurrection and the Life taught them the truth and purity of his doctrine. (See Matthew 22:23—33.)

As a last attempt, one of the scribes (those lawyers who interpreted the law of Moses) asked Jesus to tell which of their many laws and commandments was the greatest. Jesus' reply took them back through the debris of their years of interpretations to the source and foundation of the law as it was revealed to Moses: "Hear, O Israel . . . thou shalt love the Lord thy God with all thy heart, and with all thy soul, and with all thy mind, and with all thy strength: this is the first commandment. And the second is like, namely this, Thou shalt love thy neighbor as thyself. There is none other commandment greater than these" (Mark 12:29—31).

The chief priests, members of the Sanhedrin, the Pharisees, Saduccees, and scribes—all who could have taught simply and exemplified these two great commandments to the people—the Savior now openly denounced. "Woe unto you . . . hypocrites!" (Matthew 23:13). They had rejected the prophets; they had rejected him, and they held back the progress of those who were seeking salvation. He enumerated their evil practices and those of the generations they imitated. Then looking to the future, he foresaw the continuation of their evil leadership after his death: "Wherefore, behold, I send unto you prophets, and wise men, and scribes: and some of them ye shall kill and crucify; and some of them shall ye scourge in your synagogues, and persecute them from city to city" (Matthew 23:34).

In this last attempt to teach them, knowing their past and all that would come upon them in the future, the Savior said, "O Jerusalem, Jerusalem, thou that killest the prophets, and stonest them which are sent unto thee, how often would I have gathered thy children together, even as a hen gathereth her chickens under her wings, and ye would not! Behold, your house is left unto you desolate" (Matthew 23:37—38).

Jesus' public teaching had drawn to a close. The rulers had regained their temple, but it would no longer be recognized as the house of God. The Savior's final testimony seared their souls: "I am come a light into the world, that whosoever believeth on me should not abide in darkness. . . . I have not spoken of myself; but the Father which sent me, he gave me a commandment, what I should say, and what I should speak. And I know that his commandment is life everlasting" (John 12:46, 49—50).

As Jesus and the disciples were leaving the temple for the last time that day, the Twelve asked him what he meant when he taught that the temple would be left to the Jews "desolate." These magnificent buildings had been under construction for over forty years. The temple and the city of Jerusalem were the center and pride of their religion and their nation. The white marble and gold ornamentation, the beautiful gates, the courts and colonnades, the elaborately embroidered veils and the altar made this temple world famous. Yet even as Jesus and the Apostles passed by the pillars which towered over them in size, the Savior solemnly said: "Behold ye these stones of the temple, and all this great work, and buildings of the temple? . . . There shall not be left here . . . one stone upon another that shall not be thrown down" (JST Mark 13:2, 5).

As these sad words of prophecy sank into their hearts, the disciples followed their Master out of the city. They began the ascent of the Mount of Olives on the road back to Bethany. Along the way they paused to rest. They were alone now at the close of a momentous April day.

As the Twelve silently pondered the Savior's words and the view of the city and temple across from them, questions arose in their minds: When would the temple be destroyed and the Jews scattered? When would the Savior come again and the wickedness of the world end?

As they made known the thoughts of their hearts, the Savior then taught these faithful leaders about the events that would soon follow. They were to expect persecution and great trials for bearing testimony of him. The city of Jerusalem would be destroyed and there would be many wars. False prophets would arise. Some would even claim to be the Christ. Conditions in the latter days would be like the days before the Flood. No one would know the exact time of his coming. Steadfastness and faithfulness among his followers would be necessary. The gospel would be preached to all the world, then he would come the second time to end all wickedness and reign in glory over his kingdom. (See Matthew 24, 25.)

Having reassured and strengthened the Twelve with new knowledge, the Savior arose and they continued on to Bethany for the night.

In the city of Jerusalem the chief priests found little rest. Their attempts to hinder the Savior's work had again been frustrated. He had not only humiliated them, but they were unable to take him because of the crowds of people that constantly thronged him in the city. In the midst of their dilemma, they were interrupted by a visitor. To their great surprise, Judas, the apostle who was the treasurer for the Twelve, had come to them. Astonished, they listened as Judas offered to betray Jesus. Judas then asked the chief priests, "What will ye give me . . . ?" (Matthew 26:15).

Their opportunity had come. Through Judas they would be able to take the Savior "in the absence of the multitude" (Luke 22:6). Their evil hearts rejoiced as they foresaw their triumph. Now, what should they pay him? They offered him thirty pieces of silver. Judas accepted. For this sum—the sum the law mandated as the price of a slave—he sold his Savior and chose Satan as his new master. Now he must wait for the right moment to betray Jesus.

Chapter 11

"AS I HAVE LOVED YOU"

The last hours of Jesus' earthly ministry were approaching. He knew the events that must follow, and he now gave his attention and concern to the final preparation of his Apostles. They came to him inquiring about the Passover. "Where wilt thou that we prepare?" (Luke 22:9). Jesus instructed Peter and John to go into Jerusalem. He told them that upon entering the city they would meet a man carrying a pitcher of water. They were to follow him to his house and make their request known. "He shall [show] you a large upper room: . . . there make ready" (Luke 22:12).

They followed the instructions given and returned to the city. There they found the man carrying the pitcher just as Jesus had said. They made their request, and it was granted. They now made ready for the Passover meal.

On that Thursday evening, Jesus and the Twelve Apostles met together in that upper room away from the crowds and all the distractions from the outside. The Twelve were not yet aware that this would be the last meal they would eat with the Savior before his death.

The mood was somber. A heaviness filled the air. They felt disquieted and uneasy. Jesus felt the intense emotions of this hour and all that would shortly come to pass. Those whom he had called his friends, who had been ordained Apostles and who had walked at his side in preparation for all that was about to happen, were gathered there with him. He looked into their eyes and spoke from his heart with emotion. "I have desired to eat this passover with you before I suffer: For I say unto you, I will not any more eat thereof, until it be fulfilled in the kingdom of God." And he took the passover cup, and gave thanks and said, "Take this, and divide it among yourselves." This was the customary way of beginning the Passover meal. (See Luke 22:15—17; *Jesus the Christ*, p. 594.)

There was a feeling of great sadness in the heart of the Savior, and it seems that tense emotions were evident among the Twelve as they prepared for the meal. When they took their places around the table a spirit of contention arose, and the Apostles questioned among themselves even at this solemn hour who should be accounted the greatest among them. Jesus was patient with his enemies and equally patient with his friends. He demanded much from his disciples but not all at once. In affectionate rebuke the Savior again reminded them that the greatest among them was he who was willing to serve others. (See Luke 22:24—26.)

Rising from the table, the Master desired to fortify his special witnesses against the snares of the evil one. Though he felt the nearness of his own suffering, he wanted still to comfort them. In complete selflessness, he took a basin and water, and he knelt down before each one of the Twelve in turn. He washed each one's feet and wiped them with a towel.

When the Master approached Peter in this service, Peter strongly resisted, saying, "Thou shalt never wash my feet." It was a common practice for the host of a gathering to provide slaves to wash the feet of the guests. Peter did not want the Master to demean himself by performing this task. Then Jesus explained, "If I wash thee not, thou hast no part with me." With these words, Peter had a change of heart and stretched forth both feet and hands saying, "Lord, not my feet only, but also my hands and my head." Jesus patiently explained that only the feet were required. (See John 13:4—10.)

When he had finished the washing, he wanted the disciples to learn from this example. He asked them if they understood what he had done, and then he taught them saying: "Ye call me Master and Lord: and . . . so I am. If I then . . . have washed your feet; ye also ought to wash one another's feet. . . . I have given you an example. . . . Verily, I say unto you, The servant is not greater than his lord; neither he that is sent greater than he that sent him. If ye know these things, happy are ye if ye do them" (John 13:13—17). The Savior had woven the ultimate message of service and unity into this "ordinance pertaining to the Holy Priesthood, the full import of which they had yet to learn" (*Jesus the Christ*, p. 596).

The Master continued using this last time together to prepare them for his absence. He spoke with sorrow, "Verily I say unto you, One of you which eateth with me shall betray me" (Mark 14:18). Such a statement must have stunned them until they were able to pose the question that weighed so heavily in each heart: "Lord, is it I?" (Matthew 26:22). Jesus indicated that it was one of the Twelve eating with him. When Judas received his portion, he spoke from the very tongue that had already bargained for thirty pieces of silver and asked, "Master, is it I?" The response to Judas was apparently made quietly only to him: "Thou hast said" (Matthew 26:25). Then Jesus added, "That thou doest, do quickly" (John 13:27). The others did not understand that Jesus was referring to the betrayal. (See *The Mortal Messiah*, 4:31–33.)

Judas left the room to go to the Jewish rulers. He left the association of his fellow Apostles. He left the Savior. He walked out into the night into darkness.

After Judas's departure, the Apostles seemed less troubled. Jesus was also relieved. (See *Jesus the Christ*, p. 599.) He now spoke to the remaining eleven as a loving parent: "Little children, yet a little while I am with you. Ye shall seek me: and as I said unto the Jews, Wither I go, ye cannot come" (John 13:33).

Aware of the sorrow and suffering through which he alone must pass, Jesus' concern was still for others. He said to his devoted Apostles, "A new commandment I give unto you, That ye love one another; as I have loved you, that ye also love one another" (John 13:34). He told them that the way people could identify his disciples would be in their love for one another. The law of Moses required that they have mutual love among neighbors, but this new commandment encompassed a higher order of love. They were to love each other as Christ had loved them. This would distinguish them and all people in any time as true disciples.

It was Peter who then asked the Lord where he was going and was told that he could not follow now. Peter anxiously asked why not. He said he would lay down his life for the Savior. He firmly declared he would go into prison or death to avoid separation from the Master. Peter was quieted by the Lord's response, "I tell thee, Peter, the cock shall not crow this day, before that thou shalt thrice deny that thou knowest me" (Luke 22:34). Peter's spirit was strong, but he did not fully understand his mortal weaknesses, which Satan desired to control.

While Jesus sat at the table with the Apostles, he took some bread, and when he had blessed it, he broke it in pieces and passed it to them saying, "Take, eat; this is in remembrance of my body which I give a ransom for you." He then took a cup and gave thanks and passed it to them saying, "Drink ye all of it. For this is in remembrance of my blood of the new testament, which is shed for as many as shall believe on my name, for the remission of their sins" (JST Matthew 26:22–24).

In this simple, reverent manner the Savior introduced the ordinance of the sacrament. Consecrated by prayer, the emblems of the Lord's body and blood were thereafter to be partaken of reverently in remembrance of him.

The eleven were sorrowful and troubled. The Master sensed their anxiety. He told them to be of good cheer. He spoke peace and comfort to them while his own heart was carrying the awful burden of that which he, in full control, was willing to endure because of his great love for all mankind. He taught them and comforted them. "Let not your heart be troubled: ye believe in God, believe also in me." He wanted them to know something of their future heavenly state and for a moment gave them a glimpse beyond the veil of the joy of associating with him eternally. "In my Father's house are many mansions: if it were not so, I would have told you. I go to prepare a place for you. And if I go and prepare a place for you, I will come again, and receive you unto myself; that where I am, there ye may be also. And whither I go ye know, and the way ye know" (John 14:1—4).

Thomas ventured to ask, "Lord, we know not whither thou goest; and how can we know the way?" The Lord told them yet another time in patience and reaffirmation, "I am the way, the truth, and the life: no man cometh unto the Father, but by me" (John 14:5—6). The way was clear. He was saying to them again as in times past, "Come, follow me."

The final instruction continued. In the simplest of terms, he expressed his greatest desire for them. "If ye love me, keep my commandments" (John 14:15). Now as the hour of separation was near, the Savior, for the first time, instructed his disciples to pray to the Father in his name. Again he reassured them with simplicity. "And whatsoever ye shall ask in my name, that will I do" (John 14:13). Through the name of Jesus Christ, they could call upon the powers of heaven in all righteous endeavors.

The uncertainty and the unknown were weighing heavily on these men who had in such a few short years risen to heights of sobering responsibility. Their preparation time for so great a calling seemed so brief. The Savior responded to the feelings in their hearts and prepared them for what they could expect after his suffering and death. Even with the oppressing nearness of the hour, he spoke reassuringly. "The Comforter, which is the Holy Ghost, whom the Father will send in my name, he shall teach you all things, and bring all things to your remembrance, whatsoever I have said unto you" (John 14:26). He wanted them to know that what they did not now understand the Holy Ghost would teach them. He would not leave them comfortless or alone.

Feelings were tender and gentle. The spirit of love was full and encompassing. He spoke again, "Peace I leave with you, my peace I give unto you: not as the world giveth, give I unto you. Let not your heart be troubled, neither let it be afraid" (John 14:27). "If ye keep my commandments, ye shall abide in my love" (John 15:10). He told them he had spoken these things to them so that his joy might remain in them and that their joy might be full. "This is my commandment, That ye love one another, as I have loved you" (John 15:12). And though they could not possibly comprehend the extent of his great love for them and all of his Father's children, still they had witnessed and partaken of his example of unbounded service and total obedience. In the final demonstration of his devotion, he explained to these humble men who were called to be his special witnesses, "Greater love hath no man than this, that a man lay down his life for his friends." "Ye are my friends," he told them, "if ye do whatsoever I command you" (John 15:13−14).

Outside this upper room, the forces of evil were raging in horrible conflict against righteousness. Inside, the Savior spoke comfort and peace. Before they left, he reminded the eleven once again, "I tell you the truth; It is expedient for you that I go away: for if I go not away, the Comforter will not come unto you" (John 16:7). The Apostles were stretched beyond their level of understanding. Then Jesus said, "I have yet many things to say unto you, but ye cannot bear them now" (John 16:12). Then he promised them that the Holy Ghost would come and give them further revelation.

Jesus now spoke not to the Apostles, but to the Father in their behalf. Lifting his eyes up toward heaven, he prayed for their understanding of the Father and the mission of the Son. "And this is life eternal, that they might know thee the only true God, and Jesus Christ, whom thou hast sent" (John 17:3). He prayed that though they were in the world, they would be blessed with the strength to be kept from its evil. With unfathomable love, he prayed to his Father not only in behalf of his Apostles alone, but for all those who would believe his gospel. He asked that they would be blessed with love and unity and oneness, "as thou, Father, art in me, and I in thee, that they also may be one in us: that the world may believe that thou hast sent me" (John 17:21).

Following this prayer, they sang a hymn together; then Jesus and the eleven Apostles left the house and went out into the night. They passed through the city gate, crossed over the Kidron Brook, and walked toward an orchard of gnarled olive trees on the slope of the Mount of Olives—an orchard known as Gethsemane.

They talked as they walked together along the darkened path. Jesus told them that on that night they would all be offended because of him. Peter was quick to pledge his loyalty, saying that if all men were offended yet he never would be. Jesus told Peter again that "before the cock crow, thou shalt deny me thrice." At this solemn time, the love Peter felt for the Savior was unbounded. Nothing was too much to ask. "Though I should die with thee, yet will I not deny thee." And the other Apostles said the same. (See Matthew 26:34—35.)

As they reached Gethsemane, the garden of the oil press, eight of the eleven were asked to wait at the entrance while Jesus went on with Peter and James and John. He spoke to these three chosen Apostles. "My soul is exceeding sorrowful, even unto death: tarry ye here, and watch." Then he walked on alone. A little further into the garden he fell on the ground and prayed. Here he pleaded,

"O my Father, if it be possible, let this cup pass from me: nevertheless not as I will, but as thou wilt" (Matthew 26:38—39).

Later, Jesus returned to the three Apostles and found them sleeping. With a sorrowful heart he asked them, "Could ye not watch with me one hour?" (Matthew 26:40.) Again he asked them to watch and pray. He reminded them that the spirit is willing but the flesh is weak, and they must pray always that they be strong enough to overcome temptation.

He went away the second time and prayed saying, "O my Father, if this cup may not pass away from me, except I drink it, thy will be done" (Matthew 26:42). Again he returned to find the Apostles sleeping. He went away a third time and continued his supplication to his Father.

It was in the Garden of Gethsemane that Jesus willingly took upon himself the sins of the world. His suffering was beyond human power to endure. The crushing anguish of his physical and spiritual agony for the sins and wickedness of others caused him to tremble and bleed great drops of blood from every pore. He was the Son of God, and yet he willingly "suffered the pain of all men, that all men might repent and come unto him" (D&C 18:11).

His Father in Heaven loved his son, Jesus Christ, beyond human comprehension. Throughout all ages in the eternal worlds he had been faithful and true, always obeying and desiring to honor his Father. At this time God beheld and heard his son cry out but was willing that he suffer for us.

In that hour of agony, the Savior prayed to his Father, "Thy will be done." In the premortal existence, he had determined his course and had spoken in the council.

"Father, thy will be done, and the glory be thine forever" (Moses 4:2). He had offered himself as the Redeemer of the world. Now, in the Garden of Gethsemane, he still had his choice. But true to his promise, he kept his Father's will.

It was enough. The hour had come. Jesus arose and returned and awakened the Apostles. Solemnly he spoke: "Rise, let us be going: behold, he is at hand that doth betray me" (Matthew 26:46).

Chapter 12

THE SON OF GOD BETRAYED AND TRIED

The light from the torches and lanterns cast strange shadows on the rocks and trees and glimmered on the swords and armor of the band of Roman soldiers. The faces of the Jewish officers and servants were harsh and determined in the flickering light as the group followed Judas up the side of the ravine toward the Garden of Gethsemane.

Earlier, when Judas had left the upper room at the last supper, he had gone straight to the chief priests. The ideal time to arrest Jesus had come. The Savior was alone with the Apostles inside the city, and it was night. The Jewish leaders eagerly agreed with Judas. Quickly, they gathered a group of their own temple guards and then applied to the leader of the Roman garrison for a band of Roman soldiers to make the arrest. The Romans were concerned that there be no unusual disturbances during the Passover celebration, for there was already enough to do to keep the large population of the city and the numerous visitors at peace. The Jews' request was granted, and the soldiers were dispatched. (See Alfred Edersheim, *The Life and Times of Jesus the Messiah*, vol. 2, New York: Longmans, Green, and Co., 1904, pp. 541–42; hereinafter referred to as *The Life and Times; Jesus the Christ*, pp. 614–15.)

Judas was now to lead this group to the Savior. And should there be any question as to which one it was they were to arrest, a signal was agreed upon. Judas said, "Whomsoever I shall kiss, that same is he; take him, and lead him away safely" (Mark 14:44).

Probably having first followed Judas to the place of the last supper and finding the room empty, the Jewish officers and the soldiers now impatiently followed him up the slope of the Mount of Olives. Judas knew where he would find Jesus. He had been there often with him.

Judas rushed ahead into the Garden of Gethsemane, into the earnestness and sacredness of all that had just happened there. Approaching the Savior, he hypocritically greeted him saying, "Master, master; and kissed him" (Mark 14:45).

The soldiers followed Judas and entering the garden plainly saw the agreed-upon signal—yet, they hesitated, then stopped. Judas, suddenly uneasy, retreated and stood over with the crowd.

Jesus stepped quietly forward and asked, "Whom seek ye?"

"Jesus of Nazareth," they answered.

"I am he," said Jesus. The crowd moved backward, and many fell to the ground in fright, awed by his commanding presence.

Again the Savior asked, "Whom seek ye?"

They answered again, "Jesus of Nazareth."

Jesus replied, "I have told you that I am he." Fully aware of the need for the Apostles to remain safe, he added, "If therefore ye seek me, let these go their way" (John 18:4—8).

Having regained their sense of purpose, the officers came toward Jesus. As they advanced, the Apostles asked the Savior if they should defend him. But Jesus reminded them that if he were to ask the Father, more than twelve legions of angels would be sent to his rescue. (See Luke 22:49; Matthew 26:53.)

Peter, overcome with the danger to his Master, used his sword and struck the ear of the servant of the high priest. The Savior immediately healed the ear and said to Peter, "Put up thy sword into the sheath: the cup which my Father hath given me, shall I not drink it?" (John 18:11).

Then allowing the soldiers to bind him, the Savior said to his captors: "Be ye come out, as against a thief, with swords and staves? When I was daily with you in the temple, ye stretched forth no hands against me: But this is your hour, and the power of darkness" (Luke 22:52—53).

Just days before, Jesus had overthrown the tables of the money changers and cleansed the temple; he had openly defeated the Pharisees, Herodians, Sadducees, and scribes, declaring them "hypocrites" before all the people. Now, in the last hours of his ministry, he willingly submitted to this illegal arrest and permitted the guards to lead him away.

The Savior was taken into the city, first to Annas, the former high priest, and then to Annas's son-in-law, Joseph Caiaphus, the ruling high priest. It was Caiaphus who had convinced the Jewish Sanhedrin that the only way to rid themselves of the problems Jesus caused would be to kill him. Now at last, they had him. Arrested and bound, he stood before them.

The high priest questioned Jesus about his disciples and his doctrine in front of those members of the Sanhedrin that could be gathered at night. Jesus reminded him that he had always taught openly in the synagogues and in the temple, not secretly. One of the officers hit Jesus in the face for so answering. To this cruelty, the Savior responded with divine composure. "If I have spoken evil, bear witness of the evil: but if well, why smitest thou me?" (John 18:23.)

Now the council tried to bring witnesses who would testify against Jesus. But they had great difficulty in finding any whose testimonies would agree, and the law required that they have two. The hours lengthened and tempers shortened. Finally they found two whose testimonies reached back to the beginning of the Savior's ministry when he first cleared the temple. The Jews had clamored for a sign of his authority, and Jesus had replied by saying, "Destroy this temple, and in three days I will raise it up" (John 2:19). He referred to the temple of his body, to his death and resurrection. The Jews had never forgiven that incident, and they now interpreted his words to mean that Jesus said he would literally destroy the temple of Jerusalem. They accused him of sedition, of being a disturber of the peace and one opposed to the government.

The Savior gave no answer to all of these false witnesses. Caiaphus, impatient and frustrated, leaped up from his seat and demanded by oath a response: "I adjure thee by the living God, that thou tell us whether thou be the Christ, the Son of God."

With absolute calm the Savior answered, "Thou hast said," and testifying of what was yet future, he added, "Hereafter shall ye see the Son of man sitting on the right hand of power, and coming in the clouds of heaven."

Now all had heard the evidence, and Caiaphus cried aloud, "He hath spoken blasphemy!" Dramatically, he tore his clothing in affected horror.

Turning to the other members of the council, he said, "What further need have we of witnesses? behold, now ye have heard his blasphemy. What think ye?"

They answered, "He is guilty of death."

In the darkness of what seemed an endless night, the council adjourned with their foretaste of victory, leaving Jesus at the mercy of the guards and servants. These taunted the Savior with satanic delight, spitting in his face and hitting him. They blindfolded the victim of their brutality, and as they struck him with their hands they called out, "Prophesy unto us, thou Christ, Who is he that smote thee?" But the Savior was submissive even as they mocked his divine gifts. (See Matthew 26:63—68; Mark 14:63—65; Luke 22:63—65.)

Outside the place where Jesus was held, a small fire burned in the courtyard to ward off the night chill. While Jesus was taken before the council, Peter and John tried to stay in the vicinity of their master. (See *Jesus the Christ*, p. 630.) But even in the crowd that waited outside near the fire and among the servants of Caiaphus, Peter was recognized three times as one of Jesus' followers. "Thou also wast with Jesus of Galilee"; "This fellow was also with Jesus of Nazareth"; "Did not I see thee in the garden with him?" came their accusing voices. (See Matthew 26:69—71; John 18:26.) And as Peter, for the third time, declared, "I know not the man," he heard the crow of a cock announcing the coming of dawn. With it came the awakened realization of his own weakness and the reality that, just as this prophecy had been fulfilled, all that Jesus had said would be fulfilled. His Master would be crucified. Peter ran out into the darkness weeping. (See Spencer W. Kimball, "Peter My Brother," *Speeches of the Year*, Provo: Brigham Young University Press, 13 July 1971, pp. 1—8.)

In the early hours of the morning, on Friday, the council of Jewish leaders met again. Legally, it was required that a prisoner condemned to death receive two trials on separate days. The judges were to spend the time between the trials fasting and praying while they considered the case and the decree of the death penalty. The council conveniently bypassed this and many other legalities. (See *Jesus the Christ*, pp. 627—28; 644—48.) The council met the second time within hours of their first sitting, and those in attendance unanimously concluded again that Jesus was guilty of blasphemy and should die.

In spite of their wicked strategy, the chief priests were well aware of a major obstacle they must yet overcome. No Jewish court had the right to carry out the death penalty. The Roman governor, Pontius Pilate, must first approve it. The governor was then present in the city for the Passover. He had come from his private residence in Caesarea to Jerusalem to help maintain order during the celebration. The Jews now took Jesus bound and led him away to the judgment hall of Pontius Pilate.

Among those in the crowd who became aware that the Savior was condemned to die was Judas. Emerging from the darkness of that night, Judas was terrified as he fully understood the awful consequences of his act of betrayal. The thirty pieces of silver and the weight of his conscience became an unbearable load. He ran to the chief priest and elders. "I have sinned in that I have betrayed the innocent blood," he cried.

But they answered cunningly to escape any responsibility: "What is that to us? See thou to it; thy sins be upon thee."

With those awful words, Judas flung the thirty pieces of silver on the temple floor and ran out of the city and "hanged himself on a tree." (See JST Matthew 27:4—10; Zechariah 11:12—13.)

In the early morning, the Roman soldiers and Jewish leaders arrived at the judgment hall of Pilate with their prisoner. If the Jews entered the residence of a nonbeliever, they would defile themselves, so Pilate came out and spoke with them while the soldiers kept Jesus. The Jews were determined that Jesus should die, and they accused him before Pilate not of blasphemy, but of "perverting the nation, and forbidding to give tribute to Caesar, saying that he himself is Christ a King" (Luke 23:2). Under Roman law this charge of treason was punishable by death.

Pilate called for Jesus and questioned him. Even under such accusations, the Savior remained calm and used Pilate's questions to teach him of a higher kingdom than those reigned over by earthly kings. When Pilate asked Jesus, "Art thou a king . . . ?" Jesus answered him, "Thou sayest that I am a king. To this end was I born, and for this cause came I into the world, that I should bear witness unto the truth. Every one that is of the truth heareth my voice" (John 18:37).

Pilate returned to the waiting Jews and said, "I find in him no fault at all" (John 18:38). But the elders and scribes objected. They would not be turned away. "He stirreth up the people, teaching throughout all Jewry, beginning from

Galilee to this place" (Luke 23:5). At these words Pilate
saw an alternative. Herod Antipas, who had ordered the
death of John the Baptist, was also in Jerusalem for the
Passover celebration. Galilee was a part of Herod's juris-
diction. When Pilate had confirmed that Jesus was a
Galilean, he sent him to Herod for judgment.

Before Herod, Jesus was silent. Herod had hoped to
be entertained, to see some miracle performed—the kind
he knew Jesus had done in Galilee. But when Jesus would
not answer his questions or the further accusations of the
chief priests and scribes, Herod had Jesus dressed in a gor-
geous robe, and he and his soldiers began to mock him
and make fun of him. Through it all, the Savior still remained silent. Realizing no further pleasure from the
prisoner and hearing no charge he was willing to seriously
consider, Herod ordered Jesus returned to Pilate.

A greater crowd had been gathering at the judgment
hall of Pilate. At the Passover season it had become a custom that the Roman governor release a prisoner who had
been condemned to die, and the crowd had come to see
the custom carried out. As they waited, Jesus was returned to Pilate. Pilate now called the Jewish rulers before
him once more regarding the Savior and addressed them:
"I . . . have found no fault in this man touching those
things whereof ye accuse him: No, nor yet Herod . . . I
will therefore chastise him, and release him."

Pilate hoped to be able to release Jesus and pardon
him as was the custom. But the chief priests and other
Jewish leaders, moving through the crowd, incited them
to reject Jesus as their choice for pardon, and they shouted
together, "Release unto us Barabbas." Barabbas was a
criminal convicted not only of seditious acts against the
Roman government but also of murder. (See Luke
23:13–18.)

Pilate was surprised and angry at the Jews for making this choice. He then asked, "What shall I do then with Jesus which is called Christ?"

The crowd cried back in answer, "Let him be crucified."

Pilate protested and questioned, "Why, what evil hath he done?"

Frenzied, their voices rose like a mighty wave, "Let him be crucified."

Reason had failed. Pilate, realizing that the crowd was becoming an uncontrollable mob, asked for a basin of water. Carefully, he washed his hands in front of the people. He was a pagan employing a Jewish symbol in hopes of influencing them. Ending the rite, he solemnly declared, "I am innocent of the blood of this just person: see ye to it."

They answered with the words that would follow them for centuries: "His blood be on us, and on our children" (Matthew 27:22—25).

Barabbas was then released, and the soldiers took Jesus to be scourged. His clothing taken away; he was tied to a column or pole and whipped. Jagged pieces of bone or metal imbedded in the whip tore at his flesh, stroke after stroke.

During the scourging, more of the soldiers had gathered to see this unusual prisoner. At its end they joined together and put a purple robe on him, a symbol of royalty. They made a crown of thorny branches and pressed it down on his head. For a scepter they put a reed into his right hand. Then laughing and taunting, they bowed before him and cried, "Hail, King of the Jews!" (Matthew 27:29). Taking the reed from his tied hands, they hit him about the head and on the crown of thorns. They slapped him and spit on him.

They stopped when Pilate once more called for Jesus. Hoping that the Jews' hearts would be softened at the sight of the brutalized prisoner and that the scourging would be punishment enough, Pilate had the Savior led before the crowd. For the third time he proclaimed Jesus innocent. But the Jewish leaders would not be robbed of their victory. They continued the demand for crucifixion and now even boldly revealed the death decree of their own council. "We have a law, and by our law he ought to die, because he made himself the Son of God" (John 19:7).

These words and the dream of warning told to him by his own wife made Pilate even more distraught. (See Matthew 27:19.) He then asked Jesus personally, "Whence art thou?" The Savior chose not to answer, and Pilate demanded, "Knowest thou not that I have power to crucify thee, and have power to release thee?" Again the Savior taught Pilate: "Thou couldest have no power at all against me, except it were given thee from above" (John 19:9–11).

Pilate returned to the Jews and met a new threat. "If thou let this man go, thou art not Caesar's friend: whosoever maketh himself a king speaketh against Caesar," they warned him (John 19:12). The accusation found its mark. Pilate knew if the Jews made any complaint about him to Rome, he could be relieved of his office, perhaps even punished for earlier crimes and injustice.

Scornfully Pilate addressed the Jews while pointing to Jesus, "Behold your King!" (John 19:14). The prisoner was then surrendered to the Jews to be crucified. Truly it was "[their] hour, and the power of darkness" (Luke 22:53).

Chapter 13

JESUS LAYS DOWN HIS LIFE

Pontius Pilate, the Roman governor, had succumbed to the pressure of the Jewish leaders and gave permission for Jesus to die on the cross. Death by crucifixion was the most horrible, painful, and degrading form of punishment the Romans used. The victims often suffered for several days, and four Roman soldiers and a centurian were ordered to guard each victim so no one would try to save them from the cross before death was complete. Roman soldiers now led the Savior along with two condemned criminals away from the judgment hall of Pilate. A crowd of people followed.

The terrible suffering in the Garden of Gethsemane; the humiliation and mental torment inflicted by the Jews all during the night; the brutal scourging by the soldiers which had torn his flesh; and Pilate's final order left Jesus greatly weakened. Yet even now, he quietly submitted himself to his tormentors as the heavy transverse beam of

the cross was placed on his shoulders, and the company
started on its way. The Savior moved with great effort
from the judgment hall toward the city gate. The Roman
soldiers became impatient and enlisted a man by the
name of Simon to carry the heavy wooden beam to the
place of crucifixion, thus hastening the evil plans that
were now unfolding.

The death procession of enemies and some friends
now moved along the path leading out of the city toward
Golgotha, the "place of a skull" (Matthew 27:33). Arriv-
ing at this place of execution on a hill overlooking the city,
the soldiers carried out their orders without delay.

It was customary among the Jews to give a man
about to die a narcotic drink for the purpose of dulling
the intense pain. When someone in the crowd passed the
drugged cup to Jesus, he refused it. He was determined to
face death with complete awareness. (See *Jesus the
Christ*, p. 655.)

Jesus allowed the soldiers to place him on a center
cross with one condemned victim on his right side and
one on his left. To secure him to the cross, spikes were
driven through his hands and feet, crushing nerves and
tendons.

At this moment, when the welfare of all mankind
for all eternity hung in the balance and there was no evidence of justice for his entire earthly ministry, Jesus still
showed concern for others. In agony and pain, after the
soldiers carried out their orders and concluded their
awful task, he spoke from the cross. Full of pity and
mercy beyond our comprehension, he prayed to his
Father for the soldiers. In their behalf, he pleaded,
"Father, forgive them; for they know not what they do"
(JST Luke 23:35).

With unwavering trust in God, his Father, and un-shakable confidence in man, a soul created in God's image, the Savior of the world, chose to be obedient and willingly carry out his earthly mission to its final end. He was fully aware that he was the only one who could pay the debt and free mankind from sin.

According to custom an inscription, prepared by order of Pilate, was placed on Jesus' cross. It was written in three languages—Greek, Latin, and Hebrew—so that it might be understood by everyone. It read, "This Is Jesus the King of the Jews" (Matthew 27:37). When the chief priests saw it, they still felt the pangs of their contest with Pilate and were also anxious about what the people might believe. They hurriedly sent representatives to the governor saying, "Write not, The King of the Jews; but that he said, I am King of the Jews." Pilate answered with finality: "What I have written I have written" (John 19:21—22).

As Jesus hung in agony on the cross, evil forces were rampant around him. The chief priests continued to discredit the Savior before the people. "If he be the King of Israel, let him now come down from the cross, and we will believe him." Satanically inspired challenges were shouted from the tongues of evil men: "He trusted in God; let him deliver him now, if he will have him: for he said, I am the Son of God" (Matthew 27:42—43). The priests and scribes mocked him and cried out, "He saved others; himself he cannot save" (Mark 15:31).

Again in these final hours of his life, Jesus overcame Satan's evil attempts to prevent him from completing his mission. He endured in dignified silence.

One of the thieves hanging on a cross next to Jesus, perhaps because of his own extreme suffering and the uncomplaining majesty of the Savior, was awakened to his divine identity. "Lord," he pleaded, "remember me when thou comest into thy kingdom." The Lord softly spoke words of comfort to him. "Verily I say unto thee, To day shalt thou be with me in paradise" (Luke 23:42—43).

During this time, Mary the mother of Jesus stood before her son at the foot of the cross. Her heart was pierced with grief and sorrow. Just over thirty years ago she had brought forth Jesus in the stable at Bethlehem. Though he was the Son of God, she had not known the pain and sorrow of the path he would follow. She now stood weeping tears of anguish. Near her in this small gathering were her sister, Mary (the wife of Cleophas), and Mary Magdalene. (See John 19:25.) The Apostle John, in thoughtful, loving service to his Master, stood with this group of devoted women at the place of crucifixion and gave them his protection.

As they stood near him, Jesus looked down from the cross. In tender compassion he saw his weeping mother and this small body of friends. He loved his mother, and because he could not care for her, he needed the help of his beloved Apostle, John. Speaking to his mother, Jesus said, "Woman, behold thy son!" And to John he said, "Behold thy mother!" (John 19:26—27). John gently led the sorrowing, grief-stricken Mary away from her dying son while the other women continued to watch from a distance. John thereafter cared for the Savior's mother as a member of his own household.

About three hours had passed since Jesus was first nailed to the cross. Now at noontime, when the sun should have been at its brightest, it was hidden. The whole earth became shrouded with a terrifying darkness.

For three more hours the Savior of the world hung on the cross and all creation mourned. (See Moses 7:56—57.)

At the ninth hour, or about three o'clock, Jesus cried out through the darkness in agony, "My God, my God, why hast thou forsaken me?" (Matthew 27:46.) The suffering in Gethsemane and the agony of the cross were now to be borne alone. In order for the Savior to receive "the glory of complete victory over the forces of sin and death," the Father temporarily withdrew his presence. (See *Jesus the Christ*, p. 661.) In that moment when God the Father might again have saved his Beloved Son, he did not interfere. His love for all mankind made it possible for him to endure the suffering of his Son. (See Bryant S. Hinckley, comp., *Sermons and Missionary Services of Melvin J. Ballard*, Salt Lake City: Deseret Book Co., 1949, pp. 154—55.)

After hanging for nearly six hours upon the cross, Jesus' body was filled with the agonizing torment of thirst, and he uttered the sole expression of his physical suffering, "I thirst" (John 19:28). Someone mercifully saturated a sponge and placing it on the end of a stalk, held it up to the Lord's lips.

Knowing that his atoning sacrifice had been accepted by the Father and that his mission was completed, the Savior submissively prayed: "Father, it is finished, thy will is done" (JST Matthew 27:54). Then with a great effort, he uttered his last words with a loud voice, "Father, into thy hands I commend my spirit" (Luke 23:46). Having said this, he voluntarily died, releasing his spirit from his body into his Father's care.

A terrifying upheaval in nature was then unleashed. A violent earthquake split the rocks. Graves were opened.

By the power of God, the veil of the temple in Jerusalem, which hung between the Holy Place and the Holy of Holies, was torn open from top to bottom, signifying the end of the Mosaic dispensation. (See *Jesus the Christ*, p. 662; McConkie, *The Mortal Messiah*, 4:229–30.)

Those present at the cross, who had mocked the Savior and were filled with anger and pride, now were suddenly sobered. Filled with fear, they hurriedly returned to Jerusalem, beating upon their chests over the terror of this event. (See Luke 23:48.)

Even the hardened Roman soldiers were awed by what had happened. One of the centurions who had watched the Savior die, exclaimed, "Truly this man was the Son of God" (Mark 15:39).

In the late afternoon, when the Jewish officials were less fearful, they began to worry about keeping their own religious laws about their Saturday Sabbath and the Passover. The land would be defiled if those who had been crucified were left on the crosses. Hastily, they went to the governor. They requested that Pilate's soldiers be allowed to use the method of breaking the victims' legs to bring about their immediate death.

Pilate having given permission, the soldiers now carried out the order. The legs of the two thieves were broken, but coming to Jesus, they found him already dead. They did not break his legs. Christ himself was the final great Passover sacrifice. He was the Firstborn; he was sinless and perfect; and though he died a terrible death, yet not a bone of his body was broken. The symbolism of the paschal lamb was complete and prophecy fulfilled. (See Exodus 12:5; Psalms 34:20; Mosiah 14:7.) As John the Baptist had proclaimed, Jesus was the perfect Lamb of God who sacrificed himself for the sins of the world.

Because they would be responsible for any irregularities, one of the soldiers, to make death certain, drove a spear into the Savior's side leaving a deep wound. Watching at a distance were a few women who witnessed with anguished hearts all that took place.

It was late on Friday, the darkest day in all the world's history. Jesus of Nazareth, the Savior of the world, was dead.

Chapter 14

ANOTHER MISSION

Pontius Pilate was again interrupted late in the day of that solemn Friday in April. The visitor's name was Joseph. His residence was in the hill country northwest of Jerusalem, in a place called Arimathea. Joseph was apparently a member of the powerful Jewish Sanhedrin, a wealthy and influential man, but also secretly a disciple of Jesus Christ. His request to Pilate was simple and straightforward. He asked permission to take the body of Jesus for burial. Pilate granted his request.

Joseph of Arimathea gave his own tomb for his Lord. It was cut out of rock and was located in a beautiful garden, not far from the place of crucifixion. Here Joseph and Nicodemus (whom Jesus had also taught) prepared the Savior's body, wrapping it in white linen with myrrh and aloes, costly spices worthy of a king. Their service was performed quickly, for the Sabbath was about to begin. Nearby, faithful women watched the preparation and planned to return after the Saturday Sabbath to bring more spices and ointments to honor their Lord. (See Luke 23:50—56; John 19:38—42.)

After Joseph of Arimathea and Nicodemus had lovingly laid the mortal body of the Savior in the tomb, and while the guards requested by the Jews kept their watch and the women anxiously waited through the Sabbath, Jesus continued his mission.

At the time of the death of Jesus Christ, there was a great company of spirits assembled together in the spirit world. His mission was now to them. These were those who had lived and died on the earth, who had listened to the prophets and gained a testimony of Jesus Christ and were faithful to it. While they lived, they had offered sacrifices, as they were taught, and they had looked forward to the time of the "great sacrifice of the Son of God" (D&C 138:12—13).

Our Father in Heaven had sent prophets and messengers to the earth since the time of Adam and Eve to teach the gospel and to tell his children of the mission of his Son, Jesus Christ, who would come. The sacrifice that the Savior would make would bless all of God's children. The Savior would overcome the power of death, so all could be resurrected—receive a renewed body and live again. The Savior would also suffer for the individual sins everyone commits. All people could be forgiven and live again with their Father in Heaven if they would obey the principles of his gospel and receive its ordinances. But there were many who lived and died on the earth who had not heard the gospel message. Some lived in places where it was not known. Many died in the flood at the time of Noah, and still others were bound by their own disobedience and died rejecting the prophets.

When someone dies, his mortal body is laid to rest, but his spirit lives on in a place called the spirit world. Now a faithful company of spirits were conversing together and rejoicing and waiting for the Savior to come to the spirit world. He alone could free them from death and bring about the resurrection.

The Savior came. He declared their liberty from the bondage of death. He taught them personally "the doctrine of the resurrection," how all mankind are redeemed from death by his sacrifice, and from their individual sins if they will repent (D&C 138:18—19).

Who can describe the joy these faithful saints felt? They had looked forward to this day with longing. Now the time had arrived, and they bowed and "acknowledged the Son of God as their Redeemer and Deliverer. . . . Their countenances shone, and the radiance from the presence of the Lord rested upon them." Filled with gratitude and love, "they sang praises unto his holy name" (D&C 138:23—24).

While these just and faithful spirits had the privilege of being in the presence of the Son of God and being taught by him, another group of spirits in the spirit world did not have this privilege. The wicked and unrepentant and the rebellious who had not accepted the message of the prophets were not able to be where Jesus was. (See D&C 138:20—21.)

With great mercy and love, the Savior organized the righteous spirits to carry the gospel message to those who were imprisoned by the darkness of disobedience or by their lack of knowledge. Just as was done in his earthly ministry, the Savior appointed messengers and gave them power and authority to carry out his work among these imprisoned spirits. (See D&C 138:30.)

Through the mission of the Savior in the spirit world, the blessings of the Atonement were made available to all mankind, "both small and great, the unrighteous as well as the faithful" (D&C 138:35). The repentant thief who had died on the cross next to the Savior, the wicked who had been taken during the flood in Noah's day, and those who had died without the opportunity to hear the gospel message—each one could now be reached by the great love of God the Father and his Son Jesus Christ. (See D&C 138:58—59; *Commentary* 1:823—24; 3:309—314.) The prophet Isaiah had seen this joyous day hundreds of years before the Savior's birth. By his ministry in the world of spirits, the Son of God carried out the commission of his Father "to bring out the prisoners from the prison, and them that sit in darkness out of the prison house" (Isaiah 42:7).

Chapter 15

"I AM THE RESURRECTION, AND THE LIFE"

The Roman soldiers had been ordered to guard the sealed tomb where Jesus' body had been placed. To neglect their duty was punishable by death. They kept their watch faithfully in the quiet of the darkness.

The terrifying events of that Friday still hung heavily over the land. Saturday had passed quietly, and now a faint streak of dawn broke through the darkness of that first great Easter morning. On this Sunday morning, while it was still dark, an angel of the Lord descended from the heavens and rolled back the massive stone, thus opening the tomb. The Roman soldiers standing guard shook with fear and fell to the ground as if they were dead. Then partially recovering, they left in terror. The tomb now stood open—and empty.

In the early dawn, Mary Magdalene, whose love and devotion had caused her to linger at the cross, now came first to the tomb. Making her way slowly through the partial darkness, she was filled with grief and sorrow. Quietly and alone, she approached the garden tomb.

Through the shadows she saw that the stone had been rolled away from the entrance of the sepulchre. In anguish she immediately went to Peter and John with fearful concern that the body of the Savior had been taken.

Peter and John shared Mary's fears and ran in haste to the sepulchre. They looked in and also found that the tomb was empty. While trying to grasp the meaning of these events, the two Apostles returned to their lodging, but Mary remained behind in the garden.

Burdened with grief, she stooped again to look into the empty tomb. There she beheld two angels in white sitting one at the head and one at the foot where the body of Jesus had lain. One of the angels spoke to her in gentle tones, "Woman, why weepest thou?" Her troubled soul responded to the haunting thought: "They have taken away my Lord, and I know not where they have laid him." With her whole heart consumed by the anxiety of the moment, she did not recognize the person standing close by. The figure spoke to her with compassion: "Woman, why weepest thou? whom seekest thou?" Thinking him the gardener, she pleaded with tears streaming down her face, "Sir, if thou have borne him hence, tell me where thou hast laid him, and I will take him away." She desired even yet to care for her Lord.

In the quiet of that garden setting, in the springtime of the year and the freshness of a new day, He spoke her name: "Mary." One word turned her grief to joy. She recognized the tone of his voice. She recognized him. Uttering the title, "Rabboni" (Master), she reached out to him. Jesus gently restrained her devotion, explaining,

"Touch me not; for I am not yet ascended to my Father: but go to my brethren, and say unto them, I ascend unto my Father, and your Father; and to my God, and your God" (John 20:13–17).

Until now no mortal person had ever beheld a resurrected being. Mary Magdalene was the first to witness this glorious event. (See *Jesus the Christ*, p. 681.) The joy in her heart carried her in great haste, eager to share the remarkable news with the others that there was no need for mourning and weeping. She delivered her message, the most significant of all recorded history — "He is risen" (Mark 16:6).

Jesus was alive. He was resurrected from the dead. She had seen him. Though her joy was great, it could not be shared, for "they . . . believed not" (Mark 16:11). This event was so extraordinary that even the Apostles, who had been carefully taught, could not yet grasp the reality of it. Millions of men had lived and died during the course of earth's history to that day, "but until that first Easter morning not one had risen from the grave." (See Marion G. Romney, "The Resurrection of Jesus," *Ensign*, May 1982, p. 6.)

Later that morning, as the sun was rising, other women came to the tomb with spices hoping to prepare the body of the Savior for final burial. They were talking as they sorrowfully walked together with timid steps, and they questioned how they would roll the stone away from the opening of the tomb. Upon reaching the tomb, they became frightened when they saw the two angels. The angels knew of their concern. One spoke to the women words of comfort, "Fear not ye: for I know that ye seek Jesus, which was crucified." He told them that Jesus was not there, that he had risen as he had said he would. He invited them to "Come, see the place where the Lord lay" (Matthew 28:5—6). He then instructed them to go quickly and tell the disciples the glorious news that the Lord had risen from the dead and that he would go ahead of them like a shepherd and meet them in their own beloved and native Galilee.

On the way to spread this glorious news, Jesus himself appeared to this faithful group of women. He greeted them, "All hail." These women, privileged above others, fell at his feet in worship. (See Matthew 28:9.) He who was dead was alive; he was actually there talking with them. He instructed them to tell the brethren to go to Galilee, and he would meet them there. The women joyously went on their way.

The Roman guards who had fled from the tomb when the angel opened it, were now in the city of Jerusalem. Under Pilate's order, they were responsible to the chief priests of the Jews for guarding the Savior's tomb. These chief priests were Saduccees whose teachings denied any belief in a resurrection. Hearing the report, they now bribed the guards with large sums of money. They were to say nothing of the angel but were to say that the disciples came while they were asleep and stole the body of Jesus so they could convince the people that he was resurrected. The soldiers accepted the bribe, and the chief priests also promised them protection if Pilate should question them. (See Matthew 28:11—15.)

In the afternoon of that first Easter Sunday, two of the disciples left Jerusalem and set out for the little town of Emmaus about seven or eight miles away. They left the city by the western gate and walked up a steady incline for some time until they reached the plateau. Behind them was the blood-stained city of Jerusalem, and the increasing

distance between them and the city seemed to bring with it
a fresher, freer atmosphere. Then leaving the paved
Roman roads, they followed gentle paths into a lovely
valley where they could see Emmaus in the distance. (See
The Life and Times, p. 639.) As they walked they spoke
with wonderment, uncertainty, and perplexity. The rulers
had crucified Jesus. Their Master, in whom they had
placed all of the hope of the future, was dead. Walking
and talking together they repeated the incomprehensible
account the women had given—that Jesus had reappeared
as a living person.

As they continued down the path, a wayfarer joined
them, and they walked on together. The stranger was
Jesus, "but their eyes were holden that they should not
know him" (Luke 24:16). Even now their faces bore evidence of their disappointment and sorrow, for they explained to the stranger that the crucified Jesus was to have
been their Messiah. Jesus walked with them through the
valley, teaching them the gospel as he had done during his
mortal ministry. As he recalled one by one the scriptures
concerning himself, fresh hope came to them. Approaching Emmaus toward evening, the two disciples did not
want to give up the comforting presence of the wayfarer,
and they invited him to tarry with them. He went in and
sat down with them for their simple evening meal. The
stranger took bread and blessed it, then breaking it, he
gave it to them.

Perhaps there was something in the earnestness of his
prayer, or in the way he broke and passed the bread, but
as "their eyes were opened" (Luke 24:31), they knew it
was Jesus himself who sat at their table. As they recognized him, he vanished from their sight. He had walked
with them, talked with them, taught them, and provided a

witness of his resurrection. His reason for joining them had been fulfilled.

The disciples were astonished and marvelled together. Then they recalled that even while their eyes were holden, their hearts had burned within them as he walked with them and taught them from the scriptures. They had experienced a witness of the Spirit from the scriptures, a reassurance of Christ's mission, and the necessity of his death and resurrection. The Savior's presence had then been a living sermon showing them what a resurrected being was like.

The two disciples immediately returned to Jerusalem to share their extraordinary experience. They found the Apostles and others meeting and worshipping together behind closed doors because of their fear of the Jewish leaders. First, the Apostles excitedly gave their joyous announcement—the Lord had risen and appeared to Simon Peter. The two disciples then told the group how the resurrected Lord had walked with them and taught them on the Emmaus road, and how in the breaking of the bread at mealtime their eyes were opened. As this group talked together giving testimony of what they had seen and heard, "Jesus himself stood in the midst of them, and saith unto them, Peace be unto you" (Luke 24:36). But they were frightened and supposed that he was a spirit because he had not entered by the door.

The Lord understood their feelings and spoke comfort to them. "Why are ye troubled? and why do thoughts arise in your hearts?" He then explained, "A spirit hath not flesh and bones, as ye see me have" (Luke 24:38–39). At his resurrection, Jesus' spirit became united with his glorified, immortal body. The two were now inseparable. He invited his disciples to touch his hands and feet. He asked them for food and ate before them. He wanted them to know that his resurrected body was tangible. (See D&C 130:22). He was a living person.

He now taught them again from the scriptures of his atonement and mission, and he taught them that his gospel would be preached among all nations. They were to be teachers and witnesses of these things. They would be assisted in their calling by the gift of the Holy Ghost and the priesthood which they held. (See John 20:22—23; Commentary 1:856—58.)

A week after this marvelous experience with the Savior, Thomas (who had been absent at the time) also had the privilege of seeing the Master, in the same setting. Then the Apostles went to Galilee to wait further instructions, as they had been directed.

They must have been refreshed in leaving the threatening atmosphere of Jerusalem to be again in their homeland among familiar scenes. While they waited for the day of their appointment, Peter told six of the Apostles that he would go fishing, probably to care for the needs of his family. Together, they fished all night, and as morning approached they were disappointed that their nets had been empty after every cast. In the early dawn as the sun was rising, Jesus stood on the shore of the Sea of Galilee and called to them asking if they had any fish. They did not recognize him. They called back saying no, they had caught none. Jesus instructed them to cast their net on the other side. They did as he said, and now they had so many fish that they were unable to draw in the nets. John quickly understood and said to Peter, "It is the Lord."

After the boat was landed, Jesus told them to bring some fish to where he had a fire burning and some bread. He invited them to come and dine with him. This was the third time Jesus showed himself to his Apostles. There could seemingly be no doubt remaining concerning his actual resurrection. (See John 21:1—14.)

Following the meal, Jesus said to Simon Peter, "Lovest thou me more than these?"—more than the great catch of fish, more than worldly things, more even than life itself? Peter answered, "Yea, Lord; thou knowest that I love thee." And the Savior said, "Feed my lambs." (See John 21:15; *The Mortal Messiah,* 4:289—90.)

The Lord repeated his question three times, "Lovest thou me?" Peter had denied the Master three times, and now it was appropriate that he should reaffirm his devotion and commitment to him three times. Each time Peter said he loved the Savior, he was directed to express his love in service: "Feed my sheep." Peter understood the instruction and was strengthened and committed now to follow the Savior even to his own martyrdom. (See John 21:15—19.)

Over a period of forty days after the time of his resurrection, the Savior continued to instruct and prepare his Apostles at various times and places. On a mountain in Galilee they were commissioned: "Go ye . . . and teach all nations, baptizing them . . . [and] teaching them to observe all things whatsoever I have commanded you" (Matthew 28:19—20).

These humble men must have felt the great trust the Lord placed in them and their tremendous responsibility as they began to comprehend the magnitude of the mission to which they were ordained. But they would not labor alone. The Savior had promised them, "Lo, I am with you alway, even unto the end of the world" (Matthew 28:20). He would be with them by the power of the Spirit.

The Apostles made the return journey to Jerusalem. There they were rejoined by the Savior. The time for preparation had passed. They walked with Jesus for the last time, probably on the familiar path to the Mount of Olives. The Lord then lifted up his hands and blessed them, and while he spoke, he rose from their midst and ascended until a cloud kept him from their sight. (See Acts 1:4—9.)

Strengthened by him, these chosen Apostles, who had faithfully walked with him during his earthly ministry, were allowed to witness the ascension of the Son of God to heaven, where he would "sit down on the right hand of the Father, to reign with almighty power" (D&C 20:24). As they stood gazing upward, two heavenly personages clothed in white spoke to the Apostles. "Ye men of Galilee, why stand ye gazing up into heaven?" Then they disclosed the joyous words, "This same Jesus, which is taken up from you into heaven, shall so come in like manner as ye have seen him go" (Acts 1:11). He would return again with power and great glory at a later time to his latter-day disciples to reign in a millennial era and establish the kingdom of heaven on earth. (See *Jesus the Christ*, pp. 788—89.)

The Apostles returned to Jerusalem. Their hearts were filled with great joy at all they had experienced, and they felt ready for their responsibility. In a spirit of worship, they met together with others, including Mary, the mother of Jesus, and the little group of faithful women who had been with Jesus in Galilee and who had followed him to Jerusalem. They now awaited the fruits of the Spirit manifest in the gift of the Holy Ghost which had been promised them.

It was the time of Pentecost, a traditional feast held in celebration of the corn harvest, a time of expressing thanks to God. It occurred nine days after Christ's ascension. The Apostles were all together at this time of devotion, when "suddenly there came a sound from heaven as of a rushing mighty wind." They were all filled with the Holy Ghost. A large group of people gathered outside the house. They represented many nationalities and languages. The Apostles spoke to them as the Spirit directed, and every man heard what they said in his own language. (See Acts 2:2–11.)

There were those in the crowd with satanic promptings who could not understand this spiritual outpouring. In mocking tones they accused the Apostles of being drunk. Peter, now filled with the Holy Ghost, was without fear of any violence or threat of any kind. He taught the people of Christ. He bore witness of his resurrection. He testified in a voice of thunder, with courage and power, "Therefore let all the house of Israel know assuredly, that God hath made that same Jesus, whom ye have crucified, both Lord and Christ."

Those earnest seekers who heard the convicion and power of Peter's words felt the testimony of the Holy Ghost in their hearts. It could not be denied, and they cried out, "Men and brethren, what shall we do?" They wanted to receive the message of salvation. They were ready to be taught, and the Apostles were ready to teach. Peter, the chief Apostle, answered them and all others for all time: "Repent, and be baptized every one of you in the name of Jesus Christ for the remission of sins, and ye shall receive the gift of the Holy Ghost." (See Acts 2:36–38.)

Chapter 16

THE SHEPHERD CALLS HIS OTHER SHEEP

Hundreds of miles from Jerusalem and across the mighty ocean, there lived on the American continent a group of people who had also been taught about the life and mission of Jesus Christ. Six hundred years before the birth of the Savior, their ancestors were led away from Jerusalem by the prophet Lehi. When Babylon invaded Jerusalem (in 587 B.C.), Lehi and his family were already safely on their way to the American continent. No one in Jerusalem knew where they were or where they had gone.

The Lord blessed and loved this people. They were a part of the house of Israel, descendants of Joseph of Egypt. (See 1 Nephi 5:14.) Over the years, the gospel was taught to them with power and simplicity. There were many great prophets sent to teach them—Nephi, Mosiah, Alma, and Samuel, to name only a few. But many of the people became indifferent and would not listen. They began to believe that there would be no Christ and that the teachings about the Savior were stories and false traditions passed down from their ancestors.

The prophets pleaded with these unbelieving people. They taught of the atonement to be made by Jesus Christ. (See 2 Nephi 9:21—23; Alma 7:9—16; Mosiah 3:5—13.) Samuel foretold plainly the signs of the Savior's birth and also his death (Helaman 14:1—6, 20—27). Even after being taught and knowing what was to happen, the people willfully rebelled against God. They drove the prophets from their cities and stoned them. They persecuted the righteous who believed in Jesus Christ. In their attempt to rid themselves of these believers, they took the law into their own hands and destroyed the government and the peace of the people. (See 3 Nephi 6:18, 28—30; 7:1—5.)

At the peak of these wicked conditions, a great storm began to gather over the land. It broke on the same day that Jesus was taken to the cross and crucified in Jerusalem. The wind blew with hurricane force, while the thunder was so loud and strong that it shook the earth until it seemed it would break open. Lightning seared the darkness. The great city of Zarahemla, from which the prophet Samuel was driven because of his testifying of Jesus, was burned. Other cities were destroyed by earthquakes and their inhabitants crushed in the falling debris. The earth convulsed and shook until cracks and seams covered the face of the land both above and beneath the ground. The highways were broken up. Some cities were heaped over with earth, while others sank into the sea. Some people were carried off in the force of the whirlwinds and never seen again.

This terrible destruction took place while the Savior hung in agony on the cross. It lasted for three hours. When the earth became more stable and the wind and lightning subsided, the people who remained found themselves shrouded in darkness. The darkness was so dense that they could feel its vapor around them. They struggled to get light. No candle would flicker. No torch would give its flame. Even with their finest, driest wood they could not kindle a fire. The sun and moon and stars were hidden. There was not a glimmer of light anywhere. (See 3 Nephi 8:5—22.)

The people were left alone in the darkness for three days. Though they could not see, they could hear and feel and remember. They listened to each other weeping and mourning for their dead and crying out, "O that we had repented before this great and terrible day, and had not killed and stoned the prophets, and cast them out" (3 Nephi 8:25). They were filled with sorrow and anguish. How they wished their people could go back in time and listen and somehow change what they had done!

Then, out of the darkness, a single voice was heard over all the land. The voice described the destruction that had come upon their great cities and declared that the wicked had died because of their iniquity, because they had destroyed the government and the peace of the people, and because they had slain the righteous and stoned the prophets who had been sent to help them. (See 3 Nephi 9:2, 9—12.)

The voice then said: "O all ye that are spared because ye were more righteous than they, will ye not now return unto me, and repent of your sins, and be converted, that I may heal you? . . . Behold, mine arm of mercy is extended towards you, and whosoever will come, him will I receive. . . . Behold, I am Jesus Christ the Son of God. . . . I am the light and the life of the world. . . . I have laid down my life, and have taken it up again; therefore repent, and come unto me ye ends of the earth, and be saved" (3 Nephi 9:13—15, 18, 22).

On the morning of the fourth day, the darkness began to disperse from off the land. The noise of the lamentation of the people and the trembling and groaning of the earth became still. There was light. The people who had lived through the destruction were filled with praise and thanksgiving for their Redeemer, the Lord Jesus Christ.

Some time later, a large multitude gathered at the temple in the land Bountiful. They were conversing with each other about the great change that had taken place. As they spoke with each other, they became aware of a voice. It seemed to come from heaven. It was not a loud voice, but it caused them to tremble as it penetrated to their very souls. They could not understand the voice at first and looked to see its source. Nor could they understand it the second time. As they anxiously looked toward heaven, they heard the voice for the third time. Their hearts burned within them as they now understood these marvelous words: "Behold my Beloved Son, in whom I am well pleased, in whom I have glorified my name—hear ye him" (3 Nephi 11:7).

As they stood gazing upward, they saw a man coming down from heaven, clothed in a white robe, who came and stood in their midst. Every eye was fixed on him. No one spoke. They thought an angel had appeared to them. But as he gestured kindly toward them, he said, "Behold, I am Jesus Christ, whom the prophets testified shall come into the world. . . . [I] have glorified the

Father in taking upon me the sins of the world, in the which I have suffered the will of the Father in all things from the beginning" (3 Nephi 11:10—11).

The multitude fell to the earth after they heard these words, for they remembered that the prophets had foretold that Jesus would come and visit them after his ascension into heaven.

The Savior spoke to the people with great understanding for their feelings. He told them to arise, and he invited them to come to him to see and feel the wound in his side and the prints of the nails in his hands and feet, so they would know for themselves that he was their Redeemer and Savior. One by one, they went to him. They did see and feel, and they knew it was He of whom their prophets foretold. Then after each had witnessed for himself, they all cried out together, "Hosanna! Blessed be the name of the Most High God!" and they fell at his feet and worshipped him. (See 3 Nephi 11:12—17.)

Among this multitude of people was a righteous man named Nephi. Jesus now called him forward with eleven others and spoke to them. He instructed them about the principle of baptism by immersion. He gave them power and authority, and he commissioned them to baptize the people in his name. (See 3 Nephi 11:18—41.)

The Savior then turned to the multitude and introduced those twelve disciples to whom he had given his authority and admonished the people to follow these chosen men and to enter into the covenant of baptism.

With clarity and simplicity, Jesus taught the people many things. He sensed their anxiety about the law of Moses. He taught the transcendent power of his gospel to lift them beyond a law of specified performances to a higher plane. The law had taught that they should not commit murder, but the gospel taught them to curb even their anger. The law was written that they should not commit adultery, but the gospel opened their view to a life of fidelity, free from immoral thoughts. The law specified that one need give only as much as he received, but the gospel envisioned love offered without stipulation or limit. "Therefore those things which were of old time, which were under the law, in me are all fulfilled. Old things are done away, and all things have become new. Therefore I would that ye should be perfect even as I, or your Father who is in heaven is perfect." They were invited to live as Jesus and the Father live. (See 3 Nephi 12; D&C 93:11—14, 19—20.)

In his teachings, the Savior referred to this people as descendants of Joseph of the house of Israel. He also referred to other descendants of the house of Israel—the Jews that he had lived among and ministered to in Jerusalem, and the ten tribes who had been led away captive by the Assyrians seven hundred years before his birth. Jesus was a shepherd to all of these people, and they were his sheep. He explained that he must now fulfill his Father's commandment and leave to minister to these lost tribes of the house of Israel. (See 3 Nephi 15:12; 17:4.)

The Savior knew the people had much to learn and think about from the teachings he had given them. He asked them to return to their homes and ponder those things that he had said. He told them to pray to the Father in his name, asking to understand his words, and to prepare their minds to meet him again the next day. But as he looked at the people, they did not move. They were crying, and their faces had an expression of desire and longing. Jesus felt such compassion for them that he could not leave. He knew their desires, and voiced them for the multitude: "Have ye any that are sick among you? Bring them hither."

When he had said this, the multitude brought forward their sick and their lame, the blind and the dumb. And he healed them, every one. As they knelt before him, they "did bathe his feet with their tears" (3 Nephi 17:5—10).

The Savior then asked that they bring their little children to him. The multitude moved back and made room until all the children had gathered in the center around the Savior. Then he asked that they all kneel down on the ground. When they had all knelt, Jesus himself knelt in the midst of them and began to pray to the Father.

The people had never before experienced anything like they experienced then as they heard Jesus speak to the Father. The feelings they had were beyond ability to express. There were no words to describe the joy they felt in hearing the Savior pray to the Father for them.

When Jesus finished his prayer, he asked the multitude to arise and said, "Blessed are ye because of your faith. And now behold, my joy is full." The Savior wept as he took each little child, "one by one, and blessed them, and prayed unto the Father for them." As he finished, he wept again and said, "Behold your little ones." The people were filled with such love and faith, that they saw the heavens opened. Angels descended and encircled their children and ministered to them. (See 3 Nephi 17:20—24.)

As the Savior taught the people, he wanted them to more fully understand his mission and atonement. They were to offer the sacrifices and burnt offerings of the Mosaic law no longer. The last great sacrifice had been made. The Savior gave his life on the cross, and the law was fulfilled. Now they were to bring to him "a broken heart and a contrite spirit." (See 3 Nephi 9:19—20; 12:19.)

Thus he described the attitude of those his atonement could bless. We must first come to know of him and his gospel and to have faith in him. The growth of that knowledge within us brings an increased awareness of our sins and weaknesses and a desire to overcome them. To repent is to change our life to conform with our new understanding of the truths of his gospel. When we are contrite our heart is softened and broken open and we recognize our own personal need for a Savior.

Jesus taught the people the significance of baptism: "Ye must repent, and be baptized in my name, and become as a little child, or ye can in nowise inherit the kingdom of God" (3 Nephi 11:38). He introduced the ordinance of the sacrament to them. Through partaking of bread and water consecrated by prayer, they were to remember the sacrifice he had made for them. "And if ye do always remember me ye shall have my Spirit to be with you" (3 Nephi 18:7). Keeping the Savior's atonement and example uppermost in their minds would help them from day to day to remain obedient. They would be blessed in turn by the inspiration and protection of the Spirit.

The Savior explained further that by taking the sacrament they "witness unto the Father that ye are willing to do that which I have commanded you" (3 Nephi 18:10). The sacrament was given to help them after their baptism to continuously remember the sacrifice the Savior had made for them, to witness before God that they would keep the commandments, and to receive according to their obedience the blessings of the Spirit. (See James E. Talmage, *A Study of the Articles of Faith,* Salt Lake City: The Church of Jesus Christ of Latter-day Saints, 1974, p. 175.)

The events that took place as Jesus taught this people were more wonderful than those that took place in his ministry in Jerusalem. (See 3 Nephi 19:35—36.) The Savior gave his disciples authority to confer the Holy Ghost as well as to baptize. (See 3 Nephi 18:36—37.) He was able to teach them many things about the future— how he would gather together all the house of Israel in the latter days and restore them to their homelands, and how the gospel must be taught to all people before he would come again to the earth in glory to establish his kingdom and rule over it in an era of peace called the millennium. (See 3 Nephi 20:22, 29—30; 26:1—3.)

After these wonderful teachings were given, and before he left the people for the last time, the Savior commanded that all that they had "seen and heard" (3 Nephi 27:23) and all he had taught them should be written down and kept. The people did as they were commanded. The records were considered sacred and were carefully engraved on metal plates and preserved in safety by their prophets to come forth in a glorious future day.

Chapter 17

HE WILL COME AGAIN

In the last recorded days of his ministry, both in Jerusalem and among the Nephites, the Savior chose to direct the thoughts of his listeners to the events surrounding his second coming. Specifically, as he walked with his Apostles on the road from Jerusalem to the Mount of Olives, he taught them and comforted them, and they began to understand that his second coming would not occur in their time. It would occur after a long period of apostasy — a time when the light of the gospel would be lost from the earth. Following this period, there would be a glorious restoration of truth and authority, and then the Lord's people would begin to be gathered from all parts of the earth to their appointed places and make ready for his return.

Earlier, pointing to a fig tree growing on the sunny hillside, the Master had said: "Behold the fig tree, and all the trees; when they now shoot forth, ye see and know of your own selves that summer is now nigh at hand. So likewise ye, when ye see these things come to pass [the Apostasy, the Restoration, and the Gathering], know ye that the kingdom of God is nigh at hand." (See Luke 21:29–31; D&C 45:34–38.)

Through all these teachings, Jesus had comforted the Apostles and given them an understanding of the future that strengthened them and dispelled their fears. Now, as they walked together for the last time, he blessed them; then he ascended into the heavens. As they watched him go they became aware of two white-robed, heavenly messengers standing with them, who now gave a glorious promise to the Apostles and to all the Savior's followers of all time: "This same Jesus, which is taken up from you into heaven, shall so come in like manner . . ." (Acts 1:11).

As members of the Church of Jesus Christ of Latter-day Saints, we each have a part in that glorious promise. In the dispensation in which we now live, all must be put in place and made ready for the time of the Savior's return. This preparation is taking place both on earth and in heaven. When the Savior went to the spirit world after his death, he organized his messengers and gave them authority to teach the gospel to those who had died without a knowledge of the truth. (See D&C 138:12–37.) But those spirits must not only have the opportunity to hear and accept the gospel; they must also have the privilege to receive its ordinances. Since these ordinances can only be administered here on earth, temples are built for this sacred work.

As we go to the temples to receive these saving ordinances for ourselves and then to perform this loving service for the dead, we are privileged to assist in the work of our Father in Heaven and his Son to "bring to pass the immortality and eternal life of man" (Moses 1:39). These blessings "have never been given to any other generation since the days of Jesus Christ and the Apostles . . . You hold the keys of the destiny of your fathers, your mothers, your progenitors . . . you hold the keys of their salvation." (Wilford Woodruff, Conference Report, October 1897, p. 47.) As faithful Saints throughout the world give their time and means to establish and participate in this glorious work, the preparation for the Savior's coming is hastened on both sides of the veil.

Through the missionary effort and the sharing of the gospel message, the gathering of Israel takes place and the kingdom of God is built up. The Savior gave this parable concerning the growth of his kingdom. "Whereunto shall we liken the kingdom of God? or with what comparison shall we compare it? It is like a grain of mustard seed, which, when it is sown in the earth, is less than all the seeds that be in the earth: but when it is sown, it groweth up, and becometh greater than all herbs, and shooteth out great branches; so that the fowls of the air may lodge under the shadow of it." (Mark 4:30−32.)

In May 1844, when there were less than forty thousand Church members, Brigham Young enthusiastically reported: "The kingdom is organized: and, although as yet no bigger than a grain of mustard seed, the little plant is in a flourishing condition, and our prospects brighter than ever" (*History of the Church*, 6:354).

One hundred and thirty years later, in April 1974, President Spencer W. Kimball felt impelled to call upon the Apostles and other priesthood leaders to "lengthen their stride" and more fully take up the Savior's charge to "go . . . into all the world, and preach the gospel to every creature." He foresaw a great increase in the number of missionaries to be called. He foresaw the gospel being carried to nations where the Church was not yet established. He foresaw the use of satellites and earth stations and "inventions of which we laymen have hardly had a glimpse" to fulfill the words of the Prophet Joseph Smith, "The truth of God will go forth boldly . . . till it has penetrated every continent . . . and sounded in every ear. . . ." (See Spencer W. Kimball, "When the World Will Be Converted," *Ensign,* October 1974, p. 10; *History of the Church,* 4:540).

When the tiny mustard seed was planted on April 6, 1830, the membership of the kingdom totalled six persons. By the time Spencer W. Kimball had spent ten years in his calling as prophet, the membership of the Church reached 5,450,000, and over twenty-seven thousand missionaries were serving.

Concerning the gathering of Israel in the latter days, the Savior had revealed that before he would come again, a specific group of people, the Lamanites, would "blossom as the rose" (D&C 49:24). The gospel would be brought to them, and as they accepted it in their lives, the beauty and gifts of this people would unfold and be manifest to the world. By the 1980s, many thousands of Lamanites in North, Central, and South America and in the islands of the Pacific had heard the voice of their Shepherd and were again "numbered among his sheep." (Helaman 15:12– 13.) The ancient records that tell of the ministry of Jesus Christ to their ancestors, engraved and preserved by prophets, are being brought to them in these latter days through the Book of Mormon.

The prayers of the prophets are being answered, and this branch of the house of Israel is now "rejoicing" before the Lord, demonstrating great faith, as expressed by one who bore testimony: "I know without doubt the Book of Mormon is a second witness of the Savior, the Son of God, Jesus Christ, the head of this church. The Book of Mormon contains the fulness of the gospel and the true history of my ancestors. This people have been named Tongans by men, but I am proud when I use the name given us by the Lord—Lamanites. My skin may be brown and dark in color, but I know assuredly that my blood is pure and perfect, for it is the blood of Nephi, Lehi, Joseph, Jacob, Isaac, and Abraham." (Tonga Toutai Paletu'a, "I Couldn't Hold Back the Tears," *Ensign*, December 1975, pp. 30−31.)

The Lord loves and remembers all his children. Through the priesthood keys bestowed by Moses (D&C 110:11), who gathered Israel anciently, the early prophets of the Restoration began the preparation for the final gathering of the Jews and their return to their homeland. The Prophet Joseph Smith had asked the Lord, ". . . have mercy upon the children of Jacob, that Jerusalem, from this hour, may begin to be redeemed. . . . And the children of Judah may begin to return to the lands which thou didst give to Abraham, their father." (D&C 109:62, 64.)

When the Apostle Orson Hyde dedicated Jerusalem in 1841 for the return of the Jews, he prayed to the Lord that they might have Jerusalem for their capital and become again a "distinct nation and government." (*History of the Church*, 4:457.) In May 1948, after centuries of heartache and struggle, the creation of Israel as an independent, modern nation miraculously came about. In 1800, there were only five thousand Jews in all of Palestine. By 1980, over three million Jews had gathered to their new homeland from many parts of the earth. Truly the hand of the Lord moves among the nations.

Much of the Lord's work among the Jews is yet to be accomplished, and through the prophets of this dispensation he has revealed it: "You have a great future and destiny before you. . . . It is true that after you return and gather your nation home, and rebuild your City and Temple, that the Gentiles may gather together their armies to go against you to battle . . . ; but when this affliction comes, the living God, that led Moses through the wilderness, will deliver you, and your Shiloh [the Messiah] will come and stand in your midst and will fight your battles; and you will know him." (Matthias F. Cowley, *Wilford Woodruff,* Salt Lake City: Bookcraft, 1964, p. 509.)

The Savior himself has said of that time: "Then shall the Jews look upon me and say: What are these wounds in thine hands and in thy feet?" And he will answer: "These wounds are the wounds with which I was wounded in the house of my friends. I am he who was lifted up. I am Jesus that was crucified. I am the Son of God." (D&C 45:51–52.)

There have been and will yet be many trials associated with the work of the dispensation in which we now live. For over forty years the prophets have counseled the members of the Church to be personally prepared to provide for themselves and others in cases of emergency. Through their own preparation they will be able to serve others. This temporal preparation foresees a greater spiritual outcome—the preparation of "another people who shall live the gospel in its fulness. This people are to become 'pure in heart' . . . They shall be of one heart and one mind . . . and there shall be no poor among them . . . It is to prepare us to become like Christ" and to build Zion. (Marion G. Romney, "Living Welfare Principles," *Ensign,* November 1981, p. 93.)

Even as the Saints in recent years have experienced floods, earthquakes, tornadoes, typhoons, and other trials in many places of the world, there has been a prevailing feeling of calm among them. Priesthood holders and other members have taken action to meet needs, restore order, give comfort and encouragement, and offer faith and prayers, and those afflicted have witnessed the Lord's hand in providing them with strength and security.

After the Teton Dam burst, releasing 80 billion gallons of water that destroyed the homes, farms and stores of the people living in its path, a photographer came upon a farmer on his land. The farmland was now buried in sand and looked like a beach. But the farmer had begun to dig and had cleared a small space. He was now planting vegetable seeds and a few flowers. The soil was sandy. The frost might even come before the harvest. Why did he do it? The farmer answered simply: "The prophet said to have a garden. . . . I plan to do what the prophet said." (See Eldon Linschoten, "Personal Impressions of the Photographer: Here's How I See It," *Ensign*, October 1976, p. 95.)

Times of difficulty try the faith of all who profess to be Latter-day Saints and follow the prophets. We are walking in the well-worn paths of those who preceded us in the quest for Zion. Help and comfort are ours through sources beyond our immediate strength, just as it was for those who have gone before us. One of the early pioneers testified: "I have pulled my handcart when I was so weak and weary from illness and lack of food that I could hardly put one foot ahead of the other. I have looked ahead and seen a patch of sand or a hill slope, and I have said, I can go only that far and there I must give up, for I cannot pull the load through it. . . . I have gone on to that sand and when I reached it, the cart began pushing me. I have looked back many times to see who was pushing my cart, but my eyes saw no one. I knew then that the angels of God were there." (*Relief Society Magazine*, January 1948, p. 8, as quoted in James E. Faust, "The Refiner's Fire," *Ensign*, May 1979, p. 53.)

With infinite love, the Savior himself promises his companionship to those who labor to bring forward his great work in this dispensation. "I will go before your face. I will be on your right hand and on your left, and my Spirit shall be in your hearts, and mine angels round about you, to bear you up." (D&C 84:88.)

Long before entering this earth life, when we were in a family association with our Father in Heaven and his Son, Jesus Christ, we made promises and covenants. We chose to accept the plan of salvation and follow the Savior. By divine appointment we have come to the earth during the time of preparation for his second coming. (See Joseph Smith, *Teachings*, p. 181; John A. Widtsoe, *Utah Genealogical and Historical Magazine*, 25 October 1934: pp. 189-190; Bruce R. McConkie, "God Foreordains His Prophets and His People," *Ensign*, May 1974, pp. 71– 73.)

As we study the scriptures we understand why the prophets and leaders of all dispensations from Adam to the present have looked forward in time to this glorious age in which we now live. Through our study, we can better understand our responsibilities as disciples of Jesus Christ. We will be better prepared to proclaim and defend him and to stand as a witness for him, as we promised in the covenant of baptism. (See Boyd K. Packer, "Scriptures," *Ensign*, November 1982, pp. 51–53; Mosiah 18:8–11, 21–22.)

Just as the adversary tried before we came to this earth, he will try again to deceive us and turn us aside from our part and our place in this important time. We will not find the path easy. We will be tried and tested to the utmost in many ways. So much of what we will be able to accomplish and what we will be able to overcome will depend on following the Savior's example. We may be ridiculed for those qualities and choices that set us apart from the majority. Subtly, through the world's environment, the power of evil will work constantly to dull our sensitivity to the Spirit.

The times and ways of our temptation will test our commitment to the Savior. It will not be enough for us to recognize what is right and believe it is good; we must have the faith and courage to act. In his great love for us, our Father in Heaven has said, "You are free to choose." (See 2 Nephi 2:27; Helaman 14:30–31.) Now, daily, hourly, the choice is placed before us. Will we follow him and our Savior as we did before?

They long to bless us and sustain us in our responsibilities and in our trials. They will seek us out when all others have left us alone. The Savior gave his life for us. He suffered pain and temptations of every kind so that, having descended below all things," he "comprehends all things" (D&C 88:6) and is therefore able to help and comfort us. If we choose to follow him, he will strengthen us and lead us safely home to our Father in Heaven, to become his sons and daughters eternally, crowned with glory, immortality, and eternal life, to receive all that the Father hath. (See D&C 76:51–59; 84:37–38.)

He gently invites all to come unto him, and he turns none away. He says to us, as he said to the Nephites (3 Nephi 9:14, 17–18):

"Behold, mine arm of mercy is extended towards you, and whosoever will come, him will I receive. . . .

"And as many as have received me, to them have I given to become the sons of God; and even so will I to as many as shall believe on my name, for behold, by me redemption cometh. . . .

"I am the light and the life of the world. . . ."

INDEX

"Living water," 37
"Loaves/fishes" miracle, 58—59
"Lost sheep," 82
Love, 102
Lucifer, 1

—M—

Machaerus, 34
Manna, 61
Martha, 83, 85, 87
Mary Magdalene, 122, 130—32
Mary (mother of Jesus), 10,
    17—18, 122
Mary (sister of Lazarus), 83,
    87—88
Mary (wife of Cleophas), 122
Matthew, 44
Miracles, feeding five thousand,
    58—59
  walk on water, 59—60
  water turned to wine, 29
Money changers, 31
Moses, 6, 66
Mount of Olives, 110

—N—

Nain, 45
Nathanael, 29, 44
Nazareth, 16—17, 38—39
Nephi, 144
Nicodemus, 32—33, 73, 126—27
Noah, 4—5

—P—

Palsied man, 42
Parables, 48—50
Paschal feast, 30
Passover feast, 17, 30, 32, 43
Pentecost, 138
Perea, 82
Peter, 28—29, 39, 44, 60, 64, 66,
    101—3, 106, 111, 113—14,
    131, 135, 139
Pharisees, 7, 42, 76

Philip, 29, 44
Philip (Herod's son), 16
Pilate, 114—19, 121
Pontius Pilate. *See* Pilate
Pool of Siloam, 72, 76
Prayer, 104
Premortal life, 1—3

—R—

Revelation, 64
Roman Empire, census, 12

—S—

Sacrament, 103
Sacrificial offerings, 27
Sadducees, 7, 95
Samarian woman, 36—37
Samaritans, 35
Sanhedrin, 86
Satan, 3—4, 23—25. *See also*
    Lucifer
Savior. *See* Jesus Christ
Scribes, 95
Sea of Galilee, 39
Sealing power, keys, 66
Sermon on the Mount, 44
Seventies, 69
"Sheep, other," 81
Sheepfold, 79—80
"Shepherd" teachings, 80
Shepherds, 13
Siloam, Pool of, 72, 76
Simeon, 13—14
Simon (the Pharisee), 45—47
Simon Peter. *See* Peter
Simon Zelotes, 44
Sinners, 46
"Sower" (parable), 49—50
Spikenard, 88
Spirit world, 128—29
Star, new, 15
Storm, calming of, 51
Swine, evil spirits enter, 52—53
Sychar, 35
Synagogue, 38